The Lake Villages of Somerset

by Stephen Minnitt and John Coles

Glastonbury Antiquarian Society, Somerset Levels Project and Somerset County Council Museums Service
1996

Published by:
Glastonbury Antiquarian Society,
Somerset Levels Project and
Somerset County Council Museums Service

ISBN 0 9507122 3 X

Design: Nicholas Tweddell
Photography: Lawrence Bostock

We are grateful to the Glastonbury Antiquarian
Society and Somerset County Museums
Officer for support in the publication of this
book. We are also grateful to a number of
people who have helped us in the preparation
of the book: Neill Bonham, Lawrence
Bostock, Jane Brayne, Susan Clements,
Bryony Coles, David Dawson, John
Loveridge, Nicholas Tweddell and Anne Marie
Warfield.

Front cover: *reconstruction of Glastonbury Lake Village at the peak of activity. Drawn by Jane Brayne.*
Back cover: *excavations at the south end of Glastonbury Lake Village, 1897.*

The Lake Villages of Somerset are one of Britain's most famous groups of ancient monuments and their story is as significant today as it was 100 years ago. It is the story of determination and dedication by one man in particular who devoted much of his active life to the exploration of the Lake Villages, and his work still forms the basis of our knowledge about the Celtic Iron Age of Southern Britain. In this booklet we present an account of the Lake Villages as they are viewed today, but we begin with a brief history of their explorations.

Arthur Bulleid was born in Glastonbury in 1862 and was brought up in a family in which antiquarian interests were strong. At the age of 26 he heard about the discoveries of lake-dwellings in Switzerland, and thought that the peat moors to the north and west of Glastonbury might also contain ancient lake villages. After four years of searching the moors, at weekends and during his holidays, he at last discovered a field that was not 'at a dead level' but was covered by small mounds (fig. 1). Moles had been at work here and had brought up some fragments of pottery, a whetstone and some pieces of bone. The field, one kilometre to the north of Glastonbury and just beside the road to Godney, belonged to a friend of the Bulleid family and he generously gave it to the Glastonbury Antiquarian Society; Bulleid's father was the founder of the Society. Bulleid began work on the Glastonbury Lake Village, as it was soon named, in July 1892

and with a small team of labourers excavated for six months each year until 1898; the other six months of each year were spent at work on the many finds recovered from the site.

The Lake Village was large, covering about one hectare or 2 acres, roughly triangular in shape, and very conveniently enclosed in a large field with no ditches cut through the ancient settlement (fig. 2). Although Bulleid expected it to be of the Stone Age, or perhaps the Bronze Age, the relics he found showed that the Glastonbury Lake Village was of the Iron Age, and as work went on it became clear that this was the richest Iron Age settlement in all Britain.

Bulleid had originally planned to be a doctor but he decided to make archaeology his career once he was well into the excavations. This prospect, a life with no foreseeable regular income, was not to everyone's satisfaction and in 1898 Bulleid made the decision to abandon work on the site and to take up his medical studies once again. He did this for two reasons, the first being that his father's house was now filled to overflowing with the relics from the site, the second being that his fiancée's father would not let his daughter marry an archaeologist with no prospects. So Bulleid resumed his studies, qualified, got married (to the same girl) and set up practice at Midsomer Norton. The Antiquarian Society, principal supporter of the excavations, had established a

1. *The Glastonbury Lake Village (outlined in white). The sinuous line of a modern stream runs from the south (bottom of photo) past the Lake Village and probably marks a course of the ancient River Brue flowing north to the Bleadney Gap. Photograph courtesy of Somerset County Council Department for the Environment.*

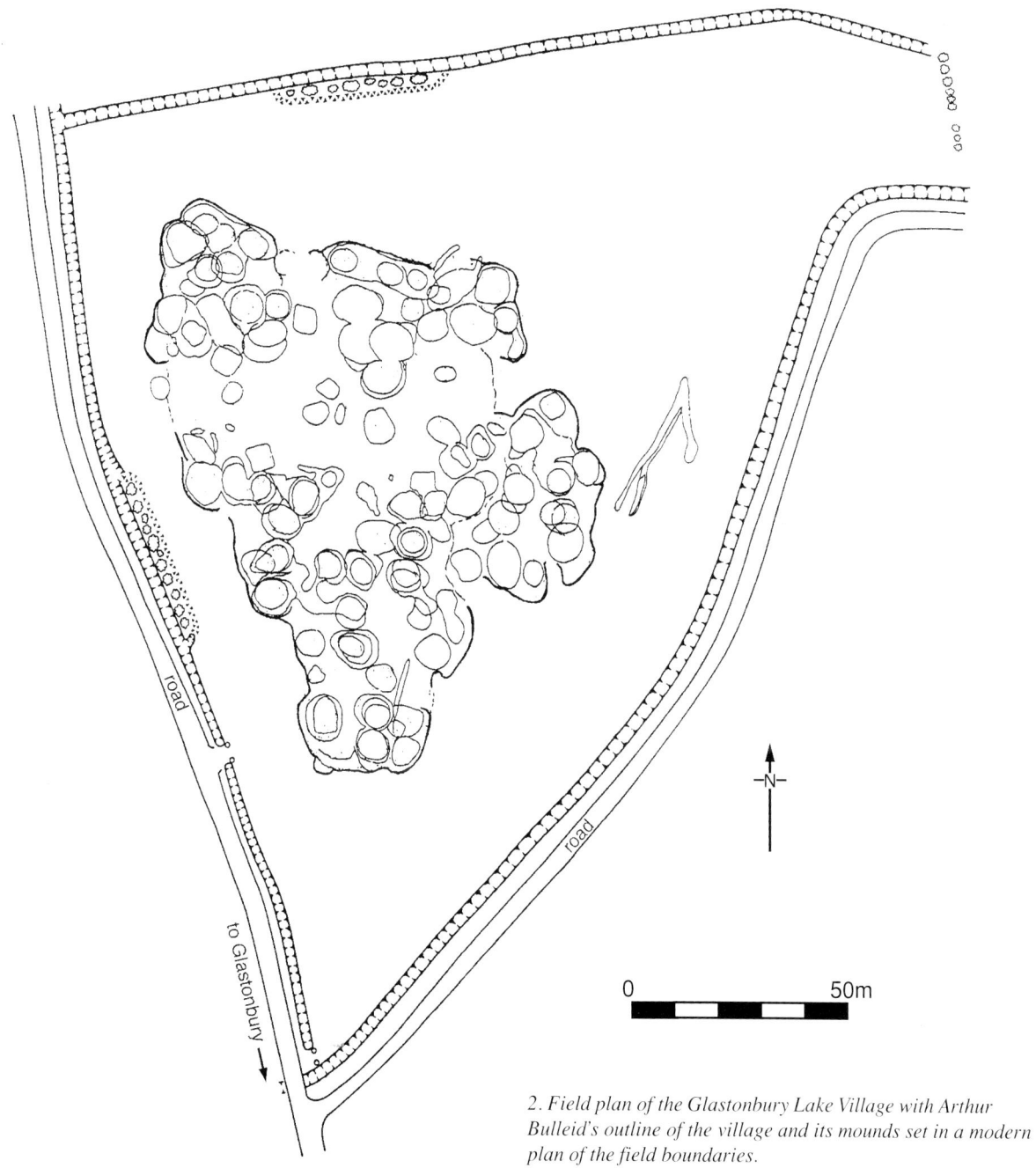

road

to Glastonbury

road

N

0   50m

2. *Field plan of the Glastonbury Lake Village with Arthur Bulleid's outline of the village and its mounds set in a modern plan of the field boundaries.*

5

museum in Glastonbury and many of the relics could be stored and displayed there. The local people were excited by the discoveries and the site brought many visitors to the town - the Abbey and the Lake Village made for a good day out.

3. Arthur Bulleid (in the hut doorway) and Harold St George Gray (right) in later life on the site of Meare Village East in 1935. With them are John Masefield (left) and Abbot Ethelbert Horne of Downside Abbey.

By 1904 Bulleid was ready to begin excavations again at the Lake Village. Now he was joined by Harold St George Gray who had been trained in the modern techniques of excavation by General Pitt-Rivers, one of the pioneers of British archaeology. Gray was Curator of the Somerset Archaeological and Natural History Society's museum in Taunton. The two men must have made a formidable

team (fig. 3), Bulleid with a strong scientific approach due to his medical training, and Gray with a good knowledge of material culture and a keen interest in the abundant relics that the labourers kept turning up as they spaded through the site. The new work went on from 1904 to 1907, and then Bulleid could write 'The systematic examination of the entire village is now complete'. The cost of the whole excavation, 1892-1907, was £697-19-0d (£697-95). Bulleid had taken no salary whatsoever and the Glastonbury Antiquarian Society had supported the work throughout. Bulleid became its president from 1908 to 1924 - a fitting tribute.

Following the completion of the excavations, Bulleid and Gray started work on the publication of the site and they managed to produce two magnificent volumes, one on the mounded site itself and some of the relics in 1911, and the other on the rest of the finds in 1917. The two books had 724 pages, 179 drawings and 101 plates - they cost 2 guineas (£2-10) and are now treasured items in many libraries.

While Bulleid was at work on the Lake Village in 1895, he received a small parcel from a farmer who lived at Westhay, just to the west of the village of Meare. The parcel contained a fragment of an Iron Age pot, a spindle whorl and a whetstone, all of the same character as those from the Glastonbury Lake Village. The note accompanying these relics said 'found when digging postholes for the rails round a haystack.' Bulleid could not get in contact with the farmer and so he went out to Westhay and searched the fields. He deduced that a farmer who had fields out on the moors would be likely to store hay on any slight mounded area, so 'it was only necessary therefore .... to examine the hay-stacks in the locality of Westhay and Meare.' This led Bulleid to the second, and the third, Lake Villages of Somerset that he called Meare Village West and Meare Village East.

the flow of mounds, separating Meare Village West from Meare Village East. Fresh from his triumphant conclusion of work at Glastonbury, Bulleid took two men to Meare Village West in 1908 and put in a trench. This yielded more objects than had been found in some of the larger Glastonbury mounds, and 'fragments of pottery and bones of animals alone filled several wheelbarrows.' The Somerset Archaeological and Natural History Society helped to organise the examination of the site and Bulleid and Gray started work in earnest, digging for a few weeks each year from 1909

4. Arthur Bulleid standing on one of the mounds at Meare Village West in 1911.

The two sites lay just off the higher land that now holds the villages of Meare and Westhay. This island in the moors is of Lias rock and is surrounded by peat, low and formerly wet. Just north of the island is a set of fields with low mounds stretching west-east for about 450 metres (fig. 4). There is a gap of 60 metres in

until 1932, excluding the World War I years. The labourers were paid 3s 6d (18p) a day, a boy helper got 1s 3d (6p) a day, until inflation set in and salaries went up to 6s 8d and 2s 6d. The day began at 7:30 am and ended at 6:00 pm, but Bulleid and Gray put in extra hours handling the finds and records. The five

7

mounded fields at Meare Village West were not fully explored, and about 30% of the settlement was left untouched.

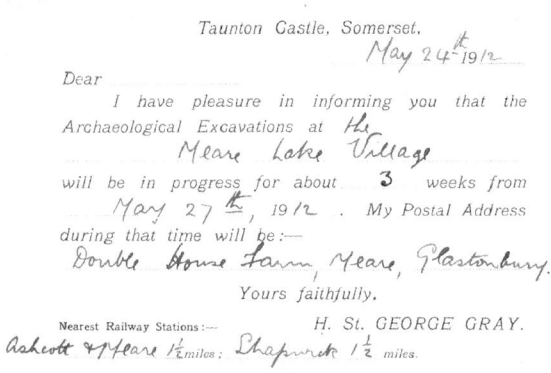

Taunton Castle, Somerset,
May 24th 1912

Dear

I have pleasure in informing you that the Archaeological Excavations at the Meare Lake Village will be in progress for about **3** weeks from May 27th, 1912. My Postal Address during that time will be:—
Double House Farm, Meare, Glastonbury.

Yours faithfully.

Nearest Railway Stations:— H. St. GEORGE GRAY.
Ashcott & Meare 1½ miles; Shapwick 1½ miles.

5. Details of each season's programme at Meare Village West were sent out to interested parties.

By 1932, Bulleid was 70 years old, and Gray was 60, but, undaunted, they embarked on their final joint excavation, at Meare Village East. Work went on until 1938 and then World War II stopped proceedings. After the War, only Gray continued at the East Village, working until 1956 when he finally gave up, aged 84. About 60% of the East Village was not excavated.

At the end Gray was still using a digging hut bought in 1910 for the Meare Villages' excavations and carefully maintained and repaired year by year (fig. 18). This hut, a three-roomed wooden building with separate offices for Bulleid and Gray, and a central storage area, was locked and left alone on one of the Meare East mounds. There it rested until 1982 when we recognised it as the original Bulleid and Gray hut. Upon entry, we saw that it still contained some of Gray's 1956 finds, some digging tools and a heap of newspapers collected for wrapping fragile objects. At the bottom of the pile was a copy of *The Times* for 1890, just when Bulleid was searching for the lake villages; at the top was *The Daily Telegraph* for 1955. The hut itself has been restored by the Somerset County Museums Service and now holds an impressive display of Bulleid and Gray's digging equipment and copies of their drawings and notebooks. (A list of Museums and other centres for display of the Lake Village finds appears at the back of this booklet.)

The work done by Bulleid and Gray at the Meare Villages, 1910-1956, was not published in such a magnificent form as was the Glastonbury Lake Village. Meare West appeared as three volumes in 1948, 1953 and 1966; by 1966 both Bulleid and Gray had died. Meare East was published in 1987. (All these books are listed at the back of this booklet).

In all this work of excavation and study, Bulleid was careful to record the observed facts as best he could; he separated his own interpretations of the Lake Villages from the bare records of the evidence. This is important because it means we can trust his record of what was seen and found, the shape of the villages, the position of the various mounds and things recovered from them. This has allowed us, and others, to try to interpret the sites. Bulleid was aware of the need to assign meanings to the evidence and he wrote a little book called *The Lake Villages of Somerset* in 1924. In this he mostly talked about the discovery of the sites and the relics found in them, but he also described the Lake Villages and their environments of 2000 years ago. The book was reprinted many times by the Glastonbury Antiquarian Society, and our booklet is designed to be its successor, bringing some new interpretations to the sites as well as describing what Bulleid and Gray found.

The Lake Villages today do not look very impressive as you approach them (fig. 1 and fig. 54). All the fields are under grass and all that can be seen are some low bumps, mostly obscured by long grass. The fields probably looked very much like this when Bulleid found them, except that the low land was probably more wet than it is today. After heavy rain, the Lake Villages can be seen much more clearly. The reason why the sites look as they did 100 years ago is because Bulleid restored the mounds as they were dug. The labourers would excavate parallel trenches, one by one, across and through the mounds, and throw the spoil from the active trench into a previous trench, storing the first trench spoil for the last trench. In this way, Bulleid could re-make the mounds to their original shape, using various poles and

measuring devices to get the correct height and diameter. Of course the mounds of today are made up of mixed material with the relics removed, and the various layers jumbled up. But because none of the Lake Village fields has been ploughed, some of the original Iron Age features remain untouched. Around the edges of the Glastonbury Lake Village are important deposits of peat of the same time as the ancient settlement, and both the Meare Villages have very extensive mounded areas not excavated. In the late 1970s and early 1980s, some excavations were carried out on all three sites to get new information which supplements that recovered by Bulleid and Gray. The Villages are still important monuments to preserve because they hold evidence that we will want to explore in the future, as new techniques of study and dating are developed.

The moors between Glastonbury and Meare are today not at all as they were during the time of the Lake Villages, about 2000 years ago. The map shows what we think conditions were like in the eastern part of the valley of the River Brue (fig. 6). The low land was, and still is, contained by the uplands to north, east and south. An ancient River Brue flowed past the Tor and turned north, becoming more of a sluggish stream than a river, as it drifted northwards through a narrow gap between Godney island and Garslade, and then flowed past Bleadney into the River Axe drainage

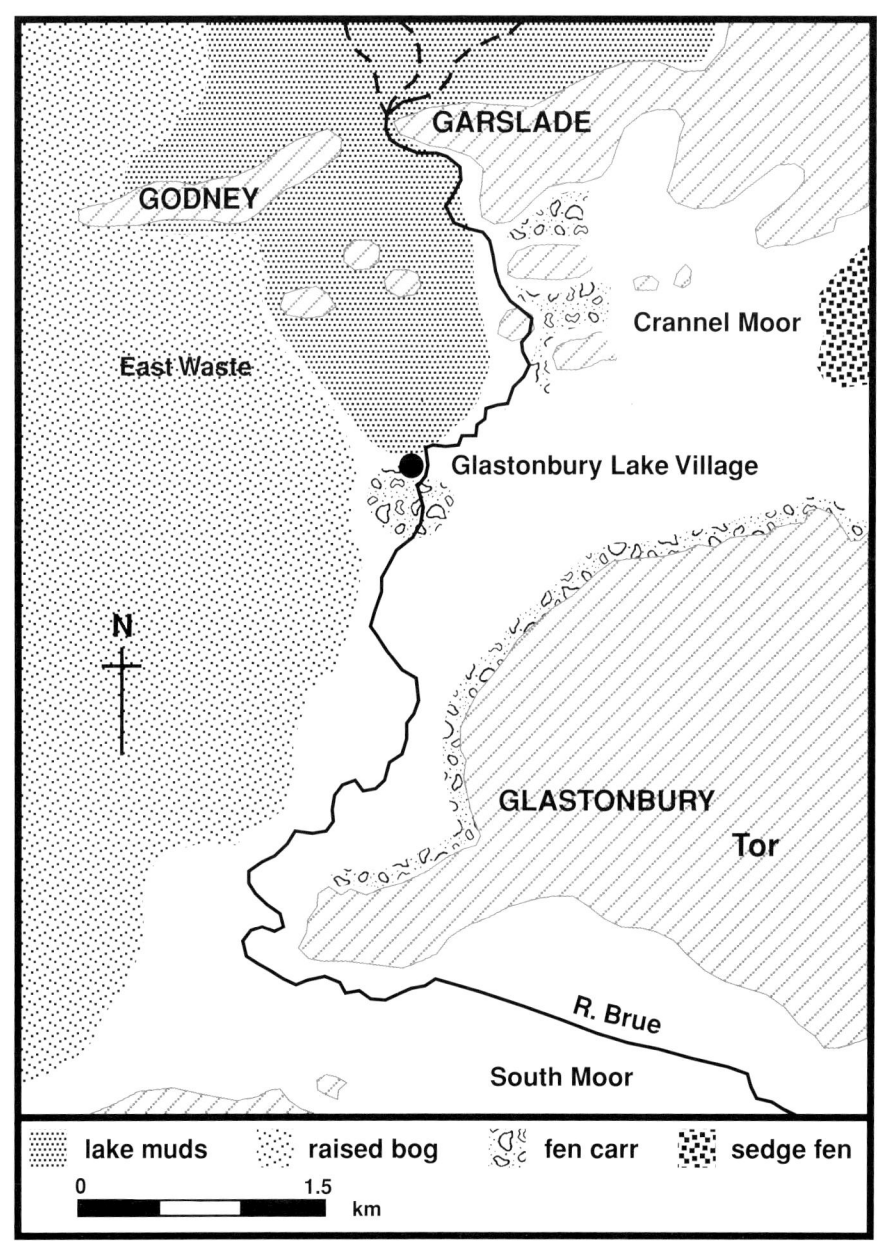

GARSLADE

GODNEY

Crannel Moor

East Waste

Glastonbury Lake Village

N

GLASTONBURY

Tor

R. Brue

South Moor

lake muds   raised bog   fen carr   sedge fen

0   1.5   km

6. The environment of Glastonbury Lake Village. The unshaded area is the great swamp through which the River Brue made its sluggish way. The hatched area is upland over 8 metres above sea level, except for the small islands which are lower.

7. View of a fen carr. The original site of Glastonbury Lake Village, before construction started, may have looked like this. Photograph by Mark Leah, Cheshire.

system. The whole area between Glastonbury and Godney was a swamp-with-trees, some patches a bit drier with birch and alder growing thickly (fig. 7), but much larger areas of reed-filled waters. To the west, the swamp was contained by a huge raised bog, a gently-domed bog of moss, cotton grass and heather that undulated and stretched westwards surrounding the rock islands of Meare-Westhay, but with at least the beginnings of a pool of open water north of Meare, later to become the medieval Meare Pool. This whole area was a desolate bog, mostly useless for human activities except for seasonal gathering of plants from the hummocks and pools of the bog surface. Perhaps some grazing of livestock could be attempted in dry seasons, but the bog was basically uninhabitable.

It will be clear from this that to call the Glastonbury and Meare sites 'Lake Villages' is inaccurate. Glastonbury was a swamp village, and the Meare sites were established on the edge of the great raised bog. None was actually a village in a lake, but their traditional names as Lake Villages are so well-fixed in all our minds that it would be silly to try to change them.

GLASTONBURY LAKE VILLAGE

The Glastonbury Lake Village as found by Bulleid consisted of a series of small and low mounds set closely together over an area of about one hectare. The mounds were the remnants of an Iron Age occupation that had once been a busy and prosperous village. After abandonment, over 2000 years ago, it had been flooded and sealed by clay and silt, then turned to grassland once drainage of the moors in recent centuries had taken effect. To understand what Bulleid and Gray found, and what their and our interpretations are based upon, we will look at one of the mounds in a little detail, beginning with the lowest deposits.

 Mound 5 (fig. 8), at the south of the village, began life with a dump of brushwood on the wet swampy surface, and with three layers of alder and oak stems or thick branches, laid crosswise to one another, the aim being to create a foundation about one metre above the dampness. Upon this was dumped some blue clay about four metres in diameter, and a small spread of extra clay. Upon this surface a few people could camp, heat food, and rest. Then more clay was brought in and placed here, to make a spread of about six by four metres. A 'primitive furnace' was made and Bulleid also noted the remains of a tuyère or bellows nozzle, and various pieces of crucible, iron and

bronze lumps. Above this floor were two further clay spreads each with a clay hearth. There was no trace of any house wall or other built structure, and these three floors were probably open-air places for metal-working or other activity. Over these was then spread a huge amount of clay, covering an area of ten by six metres, with a hearth near the centre and a set of wooden posts along the western edge and traces of other posts on the east as well. It is likely that these represent parts of an oval or rounded house. It was soon replaced, or repaired, by a new clay floor and new walls on the west. By now the whole heap of clay floors was well over one metre thick; when Bulleid excavated it the thickness was still 1.1 metres. On the various floors and around the edges of the mound there were scatters of debris, of potsherds, bone, seeds, flints, bronze and iron objects, bone tools and stone fragments.

From this short description it is clear that this place within the Village underwent substantial changes in its shape and function. Bulleid's records are not always as precise as we might wish them to be, but we can identify here three distinct phases of activity - small open-air camping place, metal-working structures and industry, domestic house. In our recent analysis of Bulleid and Gray's records we have tried to work out the sequence of events on each of the 90 mounds or spreads that they found in their excavations. We can distinguish several different kinds of structure on the Lake

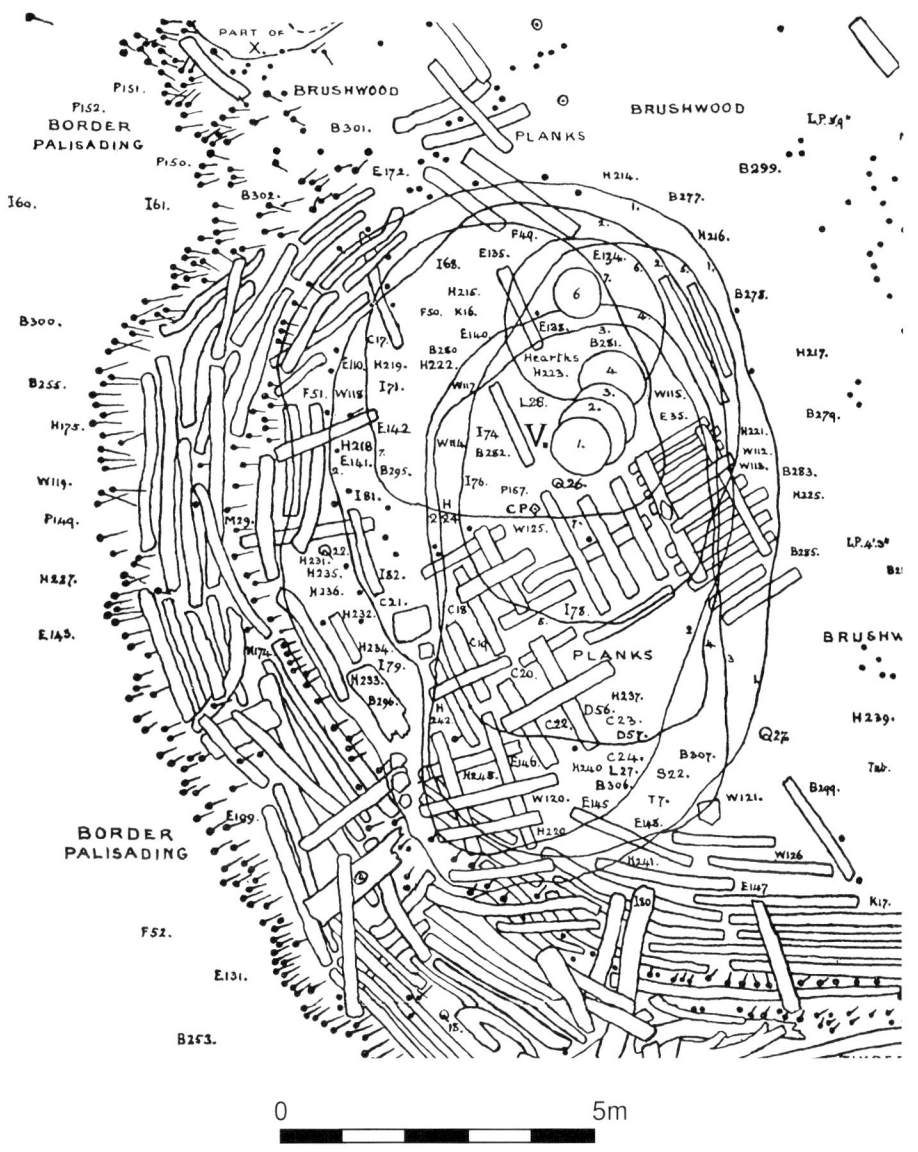

8. *Bulleid's plan of Mound 5 at Glastonbury, showing the round hearths, edges of the clay floors, angled posts of the palisade and vertical posts of walling and other structures. The artifacts were labelled by an alphabet/number system based upon the material from which they were made e.g. B 299 (bone). Note also the foundation and pathway planks*

13

Village, all designed to provide a relatively dry, sheltered and warm environment for the inhabitants.

1.The whole area of the settlement had a foundation of logs, brushwood, peat, clay, rocks, bracken and rush, dumped and arranged to make an uneven and rather wobbly surface for the clay spreads (fig. 9). Almost all this material was brought to the site from the islands or mainland around the swamp.

2.The clay floors or spreads that in effect made up the mounds ranged from a small patch only one metre or so across, to huge spreads 10 or 15 metres in length and several metres wide. Many were circular or oval, 4-12 metres in diameter. The clay came from quarries on the Glastonbury upland about one kilometre from the site, and we think at least 1000 tonnes were transported by boat or raft across the swamps. The clay might be mixed with ash to help prevent it cracking when it dried. The floors

9. Part of the heavy foundation timbers under Mound 13 at Glastonbury in 1907 and Tom Paul, Bulleid's most trusted excavator.

and spreads formed the base of open-air activity areas or the actual floors of shelters and round houses.

3.Although Bulleid believed that about 70 of the mounds at Glastonbury represented round houses, our analysis of the records suggests that there were only about 40 houses ever built during the whole occupation of the site. A round house was made by driving wall posts through a clay floor into the foundation wood, to make the circular shape (fig. 10). These posts, set 15-38 centimetres apart, were linked by slender rods woven around them or by tying woven panels to them (fig. 11). This created a wall about two metres high. The walls were then packed with clay daub both inside and out to make a heavy and windproof wall. There was a single entrance with heavy posts set to hold a solid door or a woven panel or skins or textiles. We know nothing about windows. The

11. Hurdles at Glastonbury Lake Village excavated by Arthur Bulleid.

roof was made of reed, rush, heather or straw, tied in bundles to purlins or woven panels fixed to the rafters. A small house of Lake Village type, about 5 metres diameter, would need 400 metres of hazel rods, 60-70 oak wall posts, three tonnes of daub (clay and straw and earth), three tonnes of floor clay, 20-30 long rafters, 550 metres of hazel purlins for the roof, one tonne of thatch and doubtless more bits and pieces used up in the construction. We would expect such a house to last for 30 years or so if it was kept warm and in reasonable repair. A larger house of 8 metres diameter would need a far larger supply of all these elements. On any reckoning, the Lake Villagers had to bring in vast quantities of materials, and we can envisage a busy scene, with rafts and boats arriving, cargo being off-loaded and carried or dragged to the required place of storage or assembly. Meantime, other people would be engaged in the building work.

10. Mound 74 at Glastonbury Lake Village fully exposed in 1906. The circular clay floor and central hearth can be clearly seen, with Bulleid's digging hut in the background.

12. A stone-built hearth capping a clay floor at Glastonbury. Most of the floor has been spaded away.

4.Not all clay spreads held houses, and many sheds, shelters and pens were built on the site. There were about 10 small sheds or barns, about 10 substantial unroofed shelters up to 10 metres long, various pens for animals, lines of fencing to mark off areas or to direct animal movement, and many single groups of posts that were probably used in many different ways, such as tethering animals or holding washing lines.

5.Some of the open clay spreads, most of the round houses and some of the sheltered areas had hearths. These were mostly placed at or near the centre of the clay floor of houses. Most of them were of baked clay, about one metre across and circular or oval in plan. Sometimes the hearths were of slabs of stone or of gravel (fig. 12). Most of the hearths were made by heaping the clay up a few centimetres above the floor, sometimes shaping a raised rim. In use these were baked hard and would soon begin to crack and crumble. Hearths were often repaired or replaced and a single floor might have three or more hearths associated with it. A few hearths were larger and more rectangular in shape, and one very large hearth was decorated with 67 circles impressed into its surface; we think this was actually a table rather than a hearth. Although Bulleid looked for house furniture, he found very little trace of it, only some stone seats. As some houses had timber floors laid on the clay base, it would seem that wooden seats, beds and tables would have survived had they ever existed. If they did exist, they were removed when the site was abandoned.

6.The plans of the Lake Village, carefully drawn by Bulleid, show various pathways through parts of the site, and along the south-western edge there may have been a sturdy wooden roadway, conveniently placed to receive some of the loads of clay and other materials arriving from the southern quarries. Some long and narrow clay spreads probably served as walkways, and here and there very narrow paths led out of the settlement into the reeds where perhaps the people could squat and have a few minutes of contemplation (fig. 50); no latrines were found in the village.

7.It now seems very clear that the settlement was not heavily fortified. Bulleid thought that a stout line of posts, forming a palisade, surrounded the whole site but this is not the case as his plans show. There were at least five and possibly nine gaps in the palisade. Several of these had tree-trunk blocking, others were open. The palisade itself was made up of single, double or even triple lines of alder

posts, 1.5-4.3 metres long, driven into the soft peats of the swamp. Here and there Bulleid found pieces of coarse wattle-work that linked the palisade post tops, so the Village was probably enclosed by a woven fence mostly one metre high. The fence was not evenly curved around the site but was irregular, following the edges of some of the clay spreads and was as much designed to hold the

13. A replica of a Glastonbury Lake Village house built at the Peat Moors Visitor Centre, Westhay. Photograph by Lawrence Bostock.

clay in place as to protect the site. The weight of house floors and hearths, and wall pressures, caused some of the clay floors to depress and squeeze outwards.

8. On the eastern edge of the settlement, Bulleid found a long bank of clay, rubble and wood which had been substantially remodelled at least once. It was called the Causeway and was probably a landing stage or dock for boats and rafts arriving on the site. There was

14. The Glastonbury Lake Village about 225 BC. Drawn by Jane Brayne.

probably the deepest water on this eastern side, and maybe the Villagers kept a narrow channel open through the reeds of the swamp, linking the settlement with the upland to the south.

These eight elements made up the structure of the settlement but of course there are many other aspects that relate to the houses (fig. 13) and open spreads, and to the pathways, palisade and entrances; among them are the middens or dumps of rubbish found outside the entrance, the heaps of animal bones, piles of cereals, industrial waste and other materials strewn around the site. These are considered later in this book.

One important aspect of the Village that Bulleid never got around to writing about was its evolution. The whole settlement cannot have been built on the chosen place in the swamp all at one time. It must have had a beginning, a development and an end. By using Bulleid's plans and notes we can work out where we think the first houses were built, and how the settlement expanded and how parts changed in character, an open clay spread, then a house, then again an open space, or a house rebuilt after it had burnt down, or a small open work station submerged by a much larger spread and windbreak. We believe there were over 80 of these functional changes on the site, accompanied by alterations and additions to the palisade, landing stage and entrances. The number of times that hearths

were repaired, renewed or rebuilt, and floors re-laid, is in the hundreds. The Village was rarely still and settled, but was almost always undergoing some work to cope with the wet conditions, new arrivals, or changes in the living and working practices. It is therefore almost impossible to pick one moment in the life of the Village when we could say 'the settlement looked like this for 20 years or so'. However, there was a beginning, which we can identify, then a period of minor expansion leading to a time when the Village was at its maximum size, and then an end. The chronology of the site is discussed below, but in essence we believe it existed from about 250 BC to about 50 BC, and into this time-frame we can fit our four snapshots of the Village.

In 250 BC, a small group of people came from the uplands and made their way through the swamp to a small patch where slightly drier conditions had allowed a fenwood of alder and willow to grow. The people felled the trees, brought in more wood and loads of clay, and established a hamlet (fig. 14). They built five or six houses, one of which soon burnt down, and created some spreads of clay for open-air work. Most of these spreads and houses were clustered together, with a small outlier to the north. Some fencing protected the settled areas from wind and helped hold the clay floors in place. We think that perhaps four groups, probably four extended families of mature men and women, with their children and their own

15. The Glastonbury Lake Village about 125 BC, at its maximum extent. Drawn by Jane Brayne.

parents, formed this first pioneer settlement, about 50 individuals in total.

After a few years, more people came, liked what they saw, and joined forces with the original inhabitants. They rebuilt some houses, erected another seven houses and made over 20 new clay spreads on the site. The area of the hamlet was expanded to the south and east and a landing stage for boats was built. The fence was strengthened and enlarged but the settlement was rather diffuse, families living some distance apart from one another. We think that this episode of minor expansion took about 50-60 years and the population grew to about 125; this must mean that new settlers had arrived.

By about 150 BC the settlement, still growing, had become a village and maybe for 50 more years it went through a period of active development. It reached its maximum extent, with 11 new houses built within a few years to join some of the previously-erected houses. Over 30 large new clay spreads were put down, the landing stage was totally rebuilt, and the site was enclosed by a fence with distinct entrances now marked out. Just about all of the former fenwood area was now occupied, with only one large space left clear of buildings. The population now may have reached 200, with as many as 14-15 family groups (fig. 15). Various remodellings of the village continued, new paths laid, outer fence strengthened, inner sheds and divisions placed here and there.

Many of the enormous heaps of domestic and industrial debris must belong to this episode, as we will outline below. The reinforcing of the outer fence, and the many extra dumps and spreads of clay may be an indication, however, that all was not well in the swamp. We think that there was already a slow rise in the level of the valley waters, so that damp patches became wet, dry parts of the settlement became damp, and maybe severe storms battered the west fence leading to its strengthening by a peat wall as well as wooden posts, against the waters.

By about 100 BC the settlement began to disintegrate. For the next 50 years more and more people left, abandoning their houses. Not a single new house was built although several were repaired. Much clay was brought in to raise floor levels and also to resurface the open-air working areas. The clay spreads were concentrated on the east; the western part of the village, on the windward side, was abandoned. Perhaps only 50 people survived the gradual exodus, but only for a limited time and we think that permanent, all-year-round settlement, was now at an end. The clay spreads may represent renewals for occupation only in the drier months of the year. By 50 BC even this had ended as the whole site was being washed by floodwaters. The houses collapsed, fences tilted, and loose debris was moved about by the waters (fig. 16). It was the end of the village, and it soon disappeared under flood silts and clays.

21

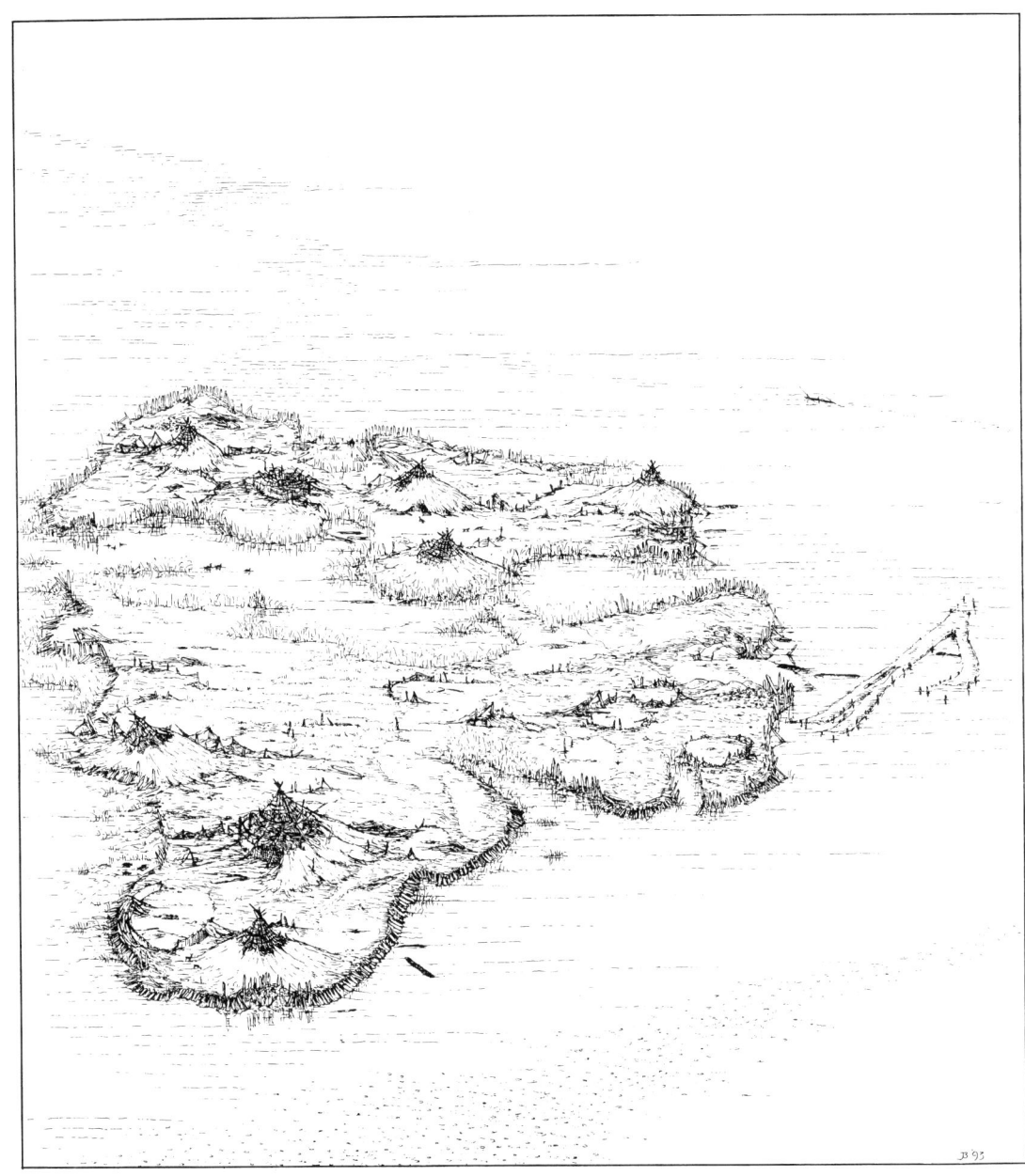

16. The Glastonbury Lake Village about 25 BC, after some years of abandonment. The houses are collapsing, the palisade is breaking-up and floodwaters surge over the site. Drawn by Jane Brayne.

17. The two Meare Villages, West and East, with the known mounds outlined. One of the modern fields at Meare West has been flattened so mounds are not now visible. The dotted lines mark the approximate edges of the two Villages.

THE MEARE VILLAGES

The story of the Glastonbury Lake Village is closely linked to the history of the Meare Villages, and before moving on to look at the domestic and industrial debris from Glastonbury, and its particularly fascinating food remains, we will turn to the west and gaze at the Meare occupations. These took place on the edge of the great raised bog that stretched, in various guises, from near the Glastonbury Lake Village to Meare and beyond. The environment of the raised bog, an uneven and undulating complex of small pools and hummocks, was made more wet than usual by the presence of a large pool of water or a very wet marsh north of the rock island of Meare; a lobe of this pool, surrounded by low domes of raised bog, extended to the very edge of the islands and probably merged with the bog lagg, the edge where water running off the bog slopes created a very wet border. Just off the island itself, and separated from it by the lagg, there were two small bog humps, high enough to be dry enough to attract people who sought such an isolated place for seasonal or periodic occupation (fig. 17). Upon the low peat surfaces, a few alder trees grew and the two humps were kept separate from one another by a very wet reed swamp, the lobe of water from the pool just to the north. So we can envisage a Meare landscape unlike that of the Glastonbury Lake Village:

1. The occupations at Meare took place on the damp and later trampled and dried-out surfaces of a raised bog, not in a tree swamp.
2. At Meare, the dry land was only 100 metres away rather than the one kilometre at Glastonbury.
3. There was no active flow of water at Meare, unlike the admittedly sluggish drifts of the Brue at Glastonbury.
4. The dried humps at Meare were periodically flooded by winter waters, whereas the Glastonbury settlers built high enough to avoid such inconvenience, at least for a time.

All in all, the occupations at Meare seem even more unstable than those at Glastonbury, and the evidence for structures is equally insecure. It may be useful here to take one of the Meare Village West mounds as an example of the site at its best in terms of structure and sequence, but at present we do not have the analytical evidence to suggest phases of settlement as we have done for Glastonbury.

Mound 7 at Meare West consisted of a thick series of clay floors, hearths and foundation wood (fig. 18). Alder stems were laid upon the raised bog surface, and then a spread of oak branches and timber capped by brushwood. This served for a time as an occupation surface and a mixture of crushed wood, churned peat, mud and other debris formed a layer of 'black earth'. Part of the area was then covered by two spreads of clay, with a hearth built on top. Lias slabs and stream pebbles were spread over the surface to try and clean it up. Over the whole area a thick clay floor was then spread, with a diameter of 5 metres, and a hearth was built and soon replaced by another. A larger clay floor was then laid down, with a hearth repaired and replaced six times; thick black earth marks some intensive occupation. Further clay floors were laid on top, with at least one hearth, and finally the whole area, now mounded, was capped by a final clay floor with a single hearth. The total for this mound was 8 clay floors and its height approached 2 metres over the original peat surface. In all of this there was little sign of wall supports and Mound 7 was probably an open work area which nonetheless received a good deal of general debris, including food

18. Mound 7 of Meare Village West in 1910, with Tom Paul standing by a deep section of superimposed clay floors and hearths. Behind is the Bulleid and Gray digging hut.

19. Bulleid's plan of Mound 13 at Meare Village West, showing the dense timberwork at the base of the mound, and several hurdles lying near the mound edge.

remains. It may have taken as many as 100 years of intermittent occupation for this sequence of deposits to accumulate.

Mound 13 was different in that it had a well-defined line of posts that must mark the wall of a round house, and it had in its foundation and adjacent a large number of hurdles as well as timber and brushwood (fig. 19). The hurdles were 1.4 metres high and 3 metres long, and woven from alder rods. The oak timber included well-carpentered beams and planks. The clay floors over this important foundation were more ordinary except for the lowest floor which had no less than eleven hearths built one on top of the other; it is tempting to think this represents annual renewals after winter abandonments of the place.

In contrast to this evidence from Meare West, the structural information from Meare East is decidedly poor, as Bulleid made clear in his notes. Mound 10 for example, was rather wide and amorphous, beginning with an occupation on the drying peat surface. Some clay hearths were made directly on the bare peat and these were later buried by a clay floor with three hearths, followed by two more floors each with one hearth. Lias rubble was dumped to enlarge the mound. There was no trace of wall posts and they are seen in only one place on those parts of Meare East excavated by Bulleid and Gray. From our reading of the records from the settlements at Meare West and Meare

East, they were unlike that at Glastonbury. Although the excavation records of Bulleid and Gray at Meare were not as good or as useful as those at Glastonbury, we can distinguish a number of interesting features as well as important differences across the sites.

1.The occupations at both Meare sites took place mostly upon the dried surfaces of raised bog, without a distinct built foundation. At Meare West, however, there were spreads of timber, hurdles, brushwood and plant stems and leaves over parts of the site. At Meare East, the debris of occupation, often called 'black earth', lay directly upon the peat and the same existed here and there at Meare West. Just as at Glastonbury, however, there were occasional square-built frames lying low down, perhaps the bases of raised sheds or other small structures at both Meare West and Meare East.

2. The clay spreads or floors, so characteristic of all three Lake Village sites, were placed upon the natural dried peat surface or upon black earth occupation deposits at both Meare sites. So here and there, some activity had gone on prior to the clay deposition, but not all over the sites. The clay spreads were often circular or oval, 10-13m across, but at Meare East in particular the clay sometimes was spread more widely over the peat, quite clearly not representing discrete stances or separate places of occupation.

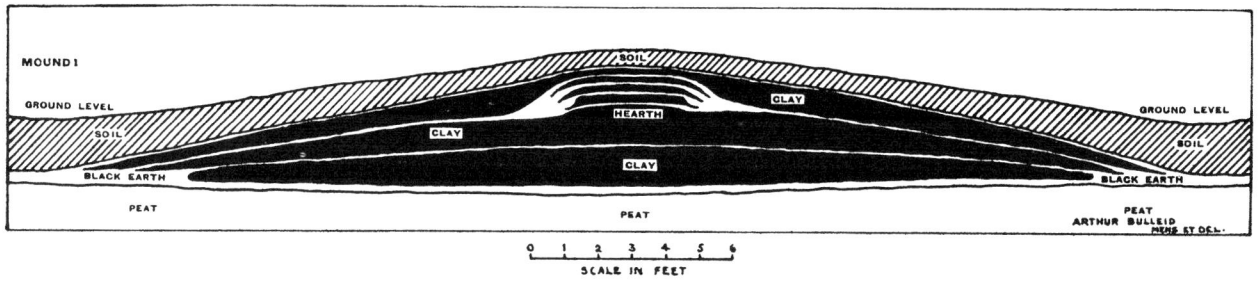

20. Section, drawn by Arthur Bulleid, through Mound 1 at Meare Village West showing the superimposed clay floors and hearths.

3. The evidence for round houses at Meare, eagerly anticipated by Bulleid and Gray, did not materialize by their excavations. In very few cases could Bulleid point to particular mounds where he was certain that houses had once existed, represented by arcs and circles of posts, fallen hurdles, central roof support, collapsed thatch, doorposts and paved entries. At Meare West, only five mounds had any kind of evidence for houses, and at Meare East there was only one place where a house might be identified.

4. At various places on both sites there were short lines of stakes or shallow arcs, as well as some settings of posts, where windbreaks or small sheds may have existed. At Meare West, the excavators found hurdles lying on the peat; these might have been fallen wall panels but more likely they were remnants of a stockpile of hurdles prepared for animal pens or fencing or windbreaks. All in all, there was little evidence for built structures of any sort at the Meare sites, and we think that the many scatters of stakes, including some in irregular arcs or even circles, were tent pegs. The settlements were in reality camps.

5. Many of the clay spreads held hearths, just as at the Glastonbury Lake Village (fig. 20). The hearths numbered at least 150 at Meare East, and probably more at Meare West; neither site was fully excavated as noted above. In many places, hearths lay on top of one another, marking renewals and replacements; many were about one metre in diameter. Hearths were often placed near the centre of the circular or oval clay spreads, and as most of the latter seem to have been open to the elements, we can envisage campfires outside the tents as well as inside them.

6. Because neither Meare West nor Meare East was fully excavated, pathways are difficult to detect but here and there the clay was spread thinly and narrowly over the peat as if to

permit drier movement between the major floors or spreads. There was no trace of any fencing or palisade around these sites, and no landing stages or visibly defined entrances to the sites. The excavations did not explore far enough outside the clay mound areas to detect such elements, but we doubt they ever existed here on these particular sites.

Unlike the Glastonbury Lake Village, the Meare settlements have not been analysed in evolutionary terms, so we cannot point to those places where occupation was first made, nor to the sequence of development of the sites. A very preliminary assessment suggests that the sites first received settlers in the decades circa 300 BC, that is 50 years or so before Glastonbury was founded. And it looks as if the early Meare occupations were scattered here and there on the two bog hummocks rather than concentrated in only one or two spots. The heavier foundations at Meare West might mark several places of the early establishment, and the mostly bog-surface occupations at Meare East might represent later settlement. We might envisage that several groups of people began to meet at Meare for a seasonal market (see below). They put up some tents and shelters, built hearths and conducted their work for several weeks each year. As the years went on , more people heard of the event, and began to come to the Meare market. New spreads of clay, hearths, shelters and tents were constructed and the

seasonal assembly grew for a time, always however dependant on the weather and winter flooding. In time, conditions deteriorated and the people abandoned the place. We think that the occupations at the Meare sites lasted until about 50 BC, the same terminal date as for Glastonbury. At Meare, almost all the mounds were covered by what Bulleid described as flood soil, a silty clay laid down by widespread flooding and still waters, essentially the first major episode of the Meare Pool of famous medieval record. The margins of the Meare settlements had driftwood and silt lying against the mound clays, and a thin layer of freshwater mussels and other shells also marked the onset of the almost total submergence of the abandoned mounds.

INDUSTRIES AND PRODUCTS

Glastonbury and the Meare sites were established on wet or damp deposits, and, during their occupations, conditions never became wholly dry. Abandonment of the sites was at least in part the result of increased wetness, inconvenient at first but cumulatively overwhelming at the end. The archaeological result of all of this softness of the sediments - the underlying peats and the organic soils and black earths formed upon them, and the sealing silts - was first, to encourage the loss of much material dropped or discarded on to the occupation surfaces, and second, to help preserve in undamaged form a wide variety of objects both man-made and of natural origin. The books of Bulleid and Gray are full of lists of things found and sometimes kept, of the discard of vast quantities of bone and wood and plain potsherds, and of the general richness of the sites for Iron Age artifacts.

The enormous quantity and variety of objects from Meare and Glastonbury provide a particularly detailed insight into the personal, industrial and craft life of the late Iron Age. Some objects had been left in situ when no longer required, perhaps sealed in position by the laying down of a new clay floor, some objects had been lost by their owners, others had been thrown away. Material disposed of was sometimes simply dropped within the settlements but at Glastonbury much was thrown immediately outside the palisade, especially at the southern end, providing a rich resource for the archaeologists. These deposits of rubbish comprised both artifacts and food waste. No comparable midden deposits were found at Meare where finds occurred in varying quantities across the site. Finds from house floors and work areas enable some places to be identified as the sites of very specific activities, others were less specialised with a wide range of artifacts and yet others were virtually or even totally devoid of finds.

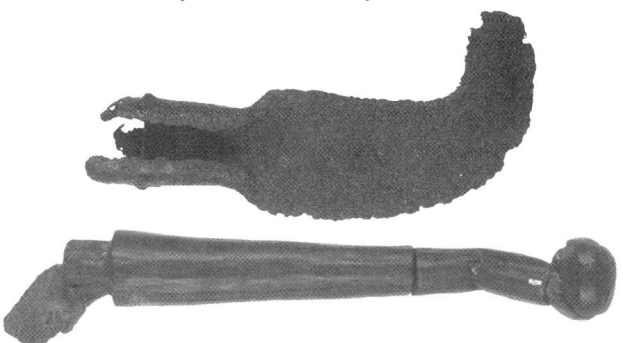

21. Billhook and sickle from Glastonbury Lake Village. Photograph by Lawrence Bostock.

This absence of finds from certain clay floors and spreads may reflect a lack of activity or it may reflect the limitations of the archaeological methods used and a failure to identify non-artifactual evidence. Certain activities, such as dye preparation, stitching of textiles and skins, carving of wood, would be archaeologically-invisible on these sites (and on almost all sites).

29

Equipment connected with production and preparation of food was found at both Meare and Glastonbury. There were iron axes and billhooks (fig. 21) which apart from on-site wood working could have been used in the clearance of land for farming. Iron sickles used in the harvest were found, one, from Glastonbury, with its wooden handle still in place. Quantities of oval-shaped baked clay sling pellets, some in hoards, were found. Slings were certainly used as weapons of war in the Iron Age, but at the Lake Villages it is

22. *Wooden ladle from Glastonbury Lake Village. Photograph by Lawrence Bostock*

likely that they were primarily for hunting. No fish hooks or fish spears were discovered but a number of flat rectangular lead weights with a hole at either end were found. These weights are interpreted as sinkers for fishing nets. The greatest number of these weights occurred at Glastonbury, almost all on the Causeway, where fishermen returning in their log boats with a catch might be expected to have landed and laid out their nets for drying or repair.

Enormous amounts of pottery were found at Meare and Glastonbury (see below). The majority of this pottery would have been used in connection with food, for cooking, storage or eating. Large coarse vessels were probably

23. *Drawing by A. Forestier, 1911, to show the Glastonbury women at work grinding corn.*

for storage. Cookpots can in some instances be recognised by traces of carbonised food still adhering to their inner surfaces. Some of the many hearths within the settlements were doubtless used for cooking and others perhaps for the smoking of meat and fish. Amongst the wooden objects from Glastonbury was a number of spoons or ladles of oak (fig. 22); some with holes in the bowl were probably strainers.

Accidentally charred wheat, barley and beans show these plants to have formed a staple part of the diet (but see below for an account of the food consumed at the Glastonbury Lake Village). Quernstones for the hand milling of grain were common finds (fig. 23). Suitable hard stone was necessary for the querns to be effective, and most were of sandstone derived from the Mendip Hills including a recently identified source on Beacon Hill, near Shepton Mallet, 15 kilometres north-east of Glastonbury Lake Village.

Pottery

One of the features of the Glastonbury and Meare Villages is the remarkable abundance of potsherds recovered from the mounds, middens and scatters across the sites. There are, in museum stores, hundreds of boxes of potsherds and most of this pottery has never been studied. Best-known are the so-called Glastonbury wares, finely-made pots bearing incised geometric and curvilinear decoration. Bulleid made a special study of these and his fine drawings grace many a book on the Iron Age of southern Britain (fig. 24). Analysis of the fabrics of Glastonbury ware has identified various sources for the clay used to manu - facture the pots; these range from Cornwall to the Mendip Hills. The clay used for most of these decorated vessels from the Lake Villages came from sources within the territory likely to be well-known to the Villagers, but a small proportion derived from Devon and Cornwall. The main local source of clay was near Shepton Mallet.

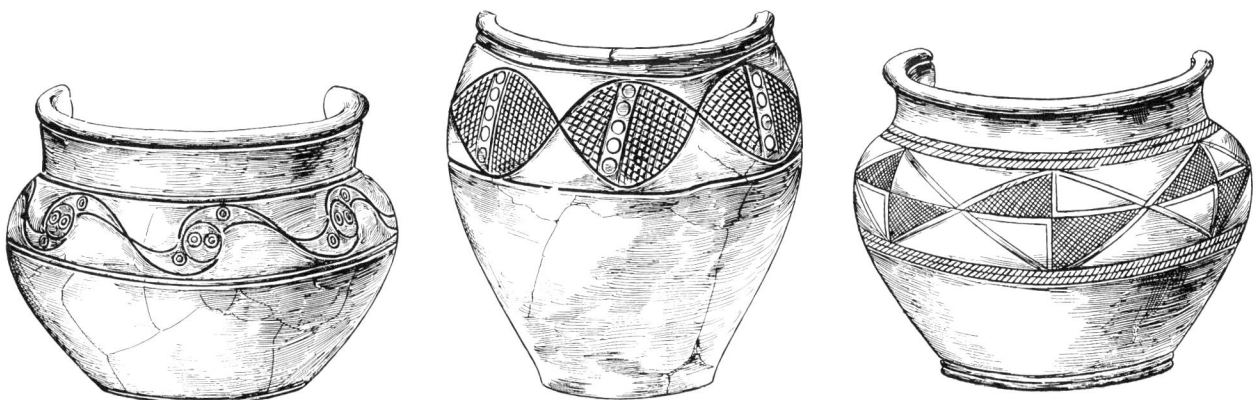

24. Three decorated pots from the Glastonbury Lake Village drawn by Arthur Bulleid.

The plain vessels, of many shapes and capacities, form about 95% of the pottery recovered by Bulleid and Gray. These wares were domestic in function, unprepossessing, utilitarian, and were easily broken and abandoned. There are very few 'wasters' on any of the three sites; these would represent the failed vessels broken or damaged in loading, firing or cooling. Wasters would point to production very close to their place of usage and disposal. If wasters are really absent from the sites, it suggests that pottery was made elsewhere and brought onto the sites. The decorated wares were certainly imported, but the huge quantities of undecorated sherds imply a large amount of labour in the transport of large and rather fragile pots; it has been estimated that as many as 50,000 pots were used and broken within the Meare Villages. Bonfire-firing was probably sufficient for most of the pottery. If not made on-site the majority of the pottery is unlikely to have been carried any great distance. Future research may well identify probable source localities for the plain pottery.

25. A ladder found just outside the palisade at Glastonbury Lake Village, perhaps abandoned there after use in thatching an adjacent house.

Wood

Wood, probably the most important of raw materials in the prehistoric period, only survives in exceptional circumstances. The permanently waterlogged conditions at Glastonbury Lake Village protected wood from the normal processes of decay. Timber survived in an enormous quantity in the foundations, as the lower posts of house walls, as complete wattlework panels and as a wide range of artifacts including containers, handles for tools of various kinds, mallets, bungs probably for leather containers, parts of wheels and even a ladder (fig. 25). We are fortunate in the survival of such discarded objects even in the archaeological environment of Glastonbury Lake Village, because when no longer required many items of wood must have ended up as fuel for the hearths.

Few wooden artifacts were found at Meare, indeed little wood of any description was found within the eastern site. Meare Village West did yield a large amount of structural, mainly foundation, timber, thousands of stakes and expanses of hurdlework, making the lack of wooden artifacts difficult to explain. An unfinished lathe-turned bowl from Meare West is an indication that wooden objects were made there.

Exposure of the wood to the air posed the excavators with immediate problems, as deterioration rapidly sct in: 'After a few hours exposure a pile (one of the palisade posts at Glastonbury) was scarcely recognisable; its fresh light colour was soon transformed to an inky-grey, and in proportion to the rapidity with which the moisture in the wood evaporated, so did the post crack longitudinally, shrink and warp, until it was about one-third of its original diameter and size.' This refers to a substantial structural timber; smaller pieces, including artifacts, were prone to even more rapid degradation unless kept wet.

Techniques for the long-term preservation of wood were not developed until relatively recently. Bulleid and Gray made no attempt to preserve any of the overwhelming quantity of structural timber, and it was either left in situ or was discarded on the spoil heaps. Some of the larger artifacts, such as the ladder, were re-

26. Wooden vessels with incised decoration from Glastonbury, a stave-built tub on the right and baskets at rear. Drawn by Sue Rouillard.

buried on-site in the hope that returning them to their original conditions below ground would preserve them for the future. The effectiveness of this decision has yet to be tested by re-excavation. A modest range of smaller wooden objects was placed in glass vessels containing a mixture of water and glycerine, and in this manner were put on display with other finds from the site in Glastonbury. The objects survived remarkably well, so much so that they successfully underwent conservation treatment 60 years later following which they no longer had to be kept immersed in liquid.

At least 16 wooden containers were found, made in a variety of ways, stave-built, lathe-turned, hand-carved and bent wood, illustrating the skill and sophistication of the Iron Age woodworker (fig. 26). Some were finely decorated with incised lines. Both Glastonbury and Meare West produced evidence for the use of baskets.

Handles for a variety of tools were found, some still attached to the tool concerned. The latter included a gouge and a saw with a blade 205 millimetres in length, both probably woodworking tools (fig. 27). The saw, in particular, had a carefully designed and carved handle. The teeth were made to cut when the saw was drawn backwards. This, like the other saws found, was small in size and could only have been used on smaller pieces of wood, a factor borne out by evidence for saw cut-marks recorded by the excavators. Larger pieces of timber were worked using axes, adzes and wedges.

There was a clear preference for oak followed by ash for working into artifacts; this contrasts with a predominance of alder and, to a lesser extent, oak, ash, willow and birch for the foundations. Timber for new structures, repairs, tools and equipment was in constant need and it is probable that some degree of woodland management was practised. The use

27. Iron saw and gouge with wooden handles from Glastonbury Lake Village. Photograph by Lawrence Bostock.

28. Drawing by A. Forestier, 1911, of the Causeway at Glastonbury Lake Village, with logboats arriving laden with swans and other products of the wetland.

of long straight rods of hazel in the making of hurdles certainly argues for the coppicing of hazel.

Amongst the wooden objects from within and near to Glastonbury Lake Village were some related to transport. The settlement was surrounded by water creating a need for some kind of boat for easy access to the site (fig. 28).

Part of a log boat of oak which measured at least 6.4 metres in length was found within the foundations; doubtless it had become unserviceable. In 1893 another log boat was found on Crannel Farm, 500 metres to the north east of Glastonbury Lake Village. Cut from a single oak trunk it measured 5.2 metres in length, 60 centimetres in width and would have been capable of transporting a load of up to one tonne. Such log boats must have been in regular use around the Glastonbury Lake Village.

29. Bronze terret ring from Glastonbury Lake Village. Photograph by Lawrence Bostock.

Evidence was also found amongst the Glastonbury woodwork for wheeled vehicles including an unfinished lathe-turned wheel hub and at least 6 spokes. The spokes averaged 35 centimetres in length with tenons at either end for fixing into wheel hub and felloe. The wheels were about 90 centimetres in diameter. No other parts of wheeled vehicles were identified except for a few bronze terret rings for guiding reins (fig. 29). We have no idea whether they used 2- or 4- wheeled carts or of the form of their super-structure. Wheeled transport would have been of limited use within Glastonbury Lake Village; the unfinished wheel hub suggests that construction or repair may have taken place within the settlement, and the various components later assembled together on the dry land where carts would be in regular use.

30. Spinning and weaving equipment from Meare and Glastonbury: spindle whorls, loom weights and weaving combs. Photograph by Lawrence Bostock.

Spinning and weaving

Sheep bones constituted the largest proportion of the animal bones found. The large quantity of spinning and weaving equipment shows that

31. Spinning wool using a spindle whorl and weaving on an upright warp-weighted loom. Drawn by Jane Brayne.

these animals were not kept for meat alone. Spindle whorls, loom weights, weaving combs and other items associated with the production of woollen cloth were found widely distributed over both Meare and Glastonbury (fig. 30). Some mounds were the site of particular activity; one mound at Meare, for example, yielded 28 weaving combs, 34 spindle whorls, 20 bone 'bobbins', 12 bone points and a quantity of baked clay loom weights. Weaving was carried out on a simple warp-weighted or upright loom (fig. 31). The vertical (warp) threads were kept taut using triangular weights made from baked clay. These weights had a restricted distribution, which must represent the places where the looms were erected. Spindle whorls, on the other hand, occurred very widely over the sites. Whorls, perforated discs made from stone, clay or bone, served as a weight on the end of a wooden spindle used for hand-spinning raw fleece into wool. The widespread distribution of whorls implies that spinning took place more or less anywhere as an activity that could very easily be picked up and put down.

Exceptionally large numbers of weaving combs were found, some with wear marks showing them to have been heavily used. Made from cut lengths of antler or bone these combs are in the region of 14 centimetres long and have between 6 and 15 teeth at one end. The

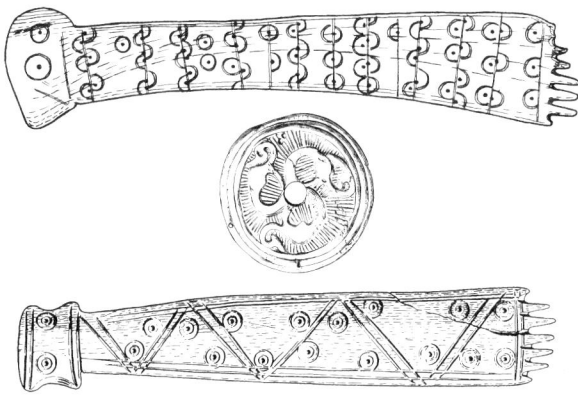

32. Items of equipment were sometimes carefully decorated such as this spindle whorl (drawn by Sean Goddard) and weaving combs from Meare Village East.

upper surface was often decorated with incised lines and circles (fig. 32). Wear patterns suggest that these combs were for making braids, ribbons or narrow strips of material for belts, straps for bags or ornamental borders.

Most Iron Age sites when excavated produce some evidence for spinning and weaving. At Meare and Glastonbury the number of spindle whorls and weaving combs is exceptional, indeed between them they have yielded about 40% of the total known weaving combs from the British Isles. The implication is that spinning and the production of braid-like fabric was carried out on an unusually large scale, beyond the residents' personal needs.

Bone and antler working

Antler and bone provided important raw materials for the production of a wide range of utilitarian and decorative items. Waste debris is clear evidence for the on-site working of these materials. Antler came mainly from red deer under 5 years old. Shed antler, as opposed to fresh antler from slaughtered animals, predominated. Utilised bone was mainly from sheep, ox and horse. Many objects have clear saw marks (fig. 33), smaller pieces were cut straight through whilst the limited efficiency of the saws meant that larger pieces often had to be cut at several points around the circumference.

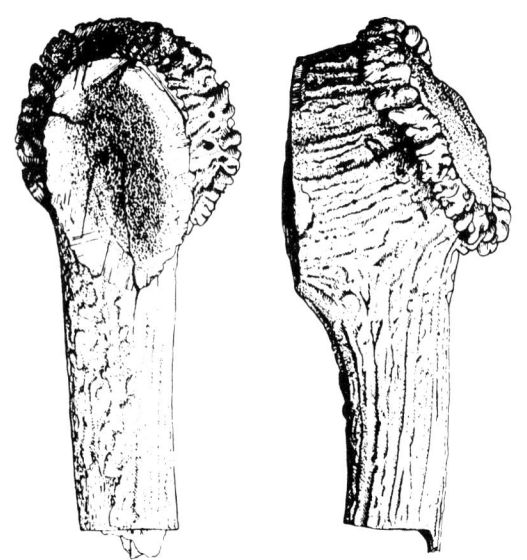
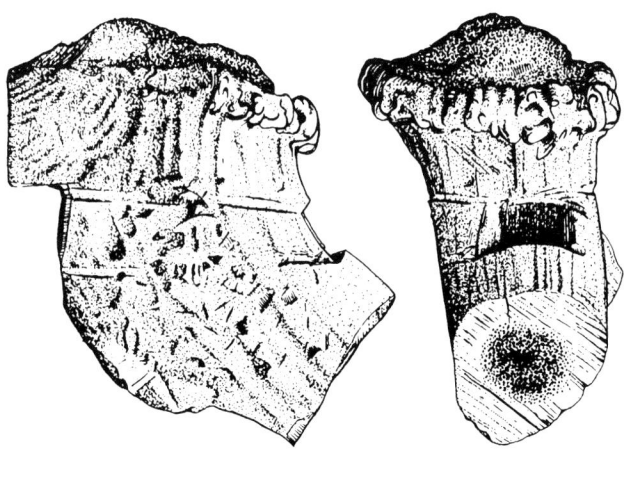

33. Pieces of sawn antler from Meare Village East. Drawn by Sean Goddard.

Amongst the objects made were various handles, hammers and hammer heads, toggles for fastening clothes, pins and needles and even dice (fig. 41). Concentrations of debris and unfinished objects have enabled the location of some bone and antler workshops to be identified on the Glastonbury and Meare sites.

Metalworking

Many Iron Age sites have produced evidence for iron and bronze working, and Glastonbury and Meare are no exception. The scale of work was modest and unlikely to have been for more than home needs. Iron was not smelted on-site; the smiths used ready smelted iron brought in as 'currency bars' (sword-shaped bars of iron) or they reworked broken or damaged objects. Iron was forged (hot worked) rather than cast as it was not possible to achieve the high temperatures necessary to melt the metal. Debris from iron working relates to the hot working of the metal and consists of smithing hearth bottoms, slag and vitrified hearth linings. Peat may have been used as fuel.

Triangular clay crucibles provide the main evidence for bronze working. Again there is nothing to indicate that smelting of copper or tin ore occurred on-site and the implication must be that recycling was the main source of metal. Bronze melts at a lower temperature

34. Drawing by A. Forestier, 1911, of bronze working at Glastonbury.

than iron, and crucibles were used to contain the metal as it was heated to melting point (fig. 34). From there it was poured into moulds. Many crucibles show clear signs of use; they were subject to high temperatures and molten metal-related deposits adhered to their surfaces. We do not know what they were casting. Just two mould fragments were found, one of clay, the other stone and both from Meare; neither was for an identifiable end product.

High temperatures were required in the metal working hearths, and these were achieved with the use of bellows. No parts of bellows were found but a number of tuyères were discovered. Tuyères were removable clay nozzles through which the air from bellows was directed into the hearth.

Several metal working sites have been identified at Glastonbury. Not surprisingly, in view of the high temperatures and potential for sparks, the activity took place in the open rather than inside a thatched building. In one case there was a windbreak or shelter associated with a metal-worker's floor - the risk of fire became a reality when this structure caught alight and burnt down. Tools belonging to a metal-worker were found - iron files and hammer heads; bronze punches may have been used to apply decoration onto metal or other materials.

Fragments of bronze sheet and rivets suggest that sheet bronze working was practised at Glastonbury, though again on a small scale. One of the most impressive and certainly best-known objects from the excavations, the 'Glastonbury Bowl', was made from sheet bronze (fig. 35). This round-bottomed vessel measures 80 millimetres in height and 123 millimetres in diameter. Made from sheet metal less than 1 millimetre thick the bowl is in two parts, the plain lower part and the upper part which has a very fine folded-over rim with fluted and punched decoration. The two sections of the bowl are joined by a horizontal row of 24 dome-headed rivets. Three further rivets were added to form a triangular arrangement at three points around the circumference. The rivets were both functional and decorative. The bowl is more likely to derive from a specialist workshop elsewhere than to have been made at Glastonbury Lake Village. However, it was well used and underwent a series of repairs, which were quite plausibly done on-site. These repairs involved rivetting on additional pieces of sheet bronze over worn or damaged areas of the base and rim; the former, in particular, was skilfully done. Doubtless a prized possession when acquired, it ended its days discarded outside the palisade.

35. The sheet bronze 'Glastonbury bowl'.
Photograph by Lawrence Bostock.

Fragments of lead ore and the unusually high number of lead and tin artifacts suggest that these metals may also have been worked. Lead would have been obtained from nearby sources on the Mendips. The tin objects from Glastonbury include a 260 millimetre-long bar of circular cross-section with bronze terminals (fig. 36). Lacking parallels and of unknown use it is rare to find such a large object made from tin.

36. Tin bar with bronze terminals from Glastonbury Lake Village. Photograph by Lawrence Bostock.

Glass

Amongst the specialists at Meare was a maker of glass beads. The workshop, with only a simple hearth, was not traced but a number of bead moulds were found. The source of the raw glass has not been identified but it may also have been produced at Meare. Evidence for glass making and working is exceedingly rare in Iron Age Europe.

Two hundred and ninety five glass beads were found at Meare, nearly 80% of which were home-produced (fig. 37). They were predominantly simple small yellow ring beads, some as little as 4 millimetres in diameter, and globular beads of colourless glass inlaid with yellow spiral, zig-zag and trellis patterns. The yellow ring beads were probably made by winding a heated glass rod around a rod of iron or bronze. A temperature of 550 degrees centigrade was necessary to make the glass sufficiently malleable. A batch of several beads could be made in one go using this method, probably the ideal way of making matching sets.

The clear glass beads with inlaid decoration were far more complex to make. They were produced in a mould which included impressions for the grooves which were to take the inlay. The regularity of the inlay, especially in the spiral decoration, shows a remarkable level of skill on the part of the maker. Inlay was achieved either by trailing a thin rod of molten yellow glass along the grooves or by covering the whole of the bead surface in yellow glass and polishing it back to the clear

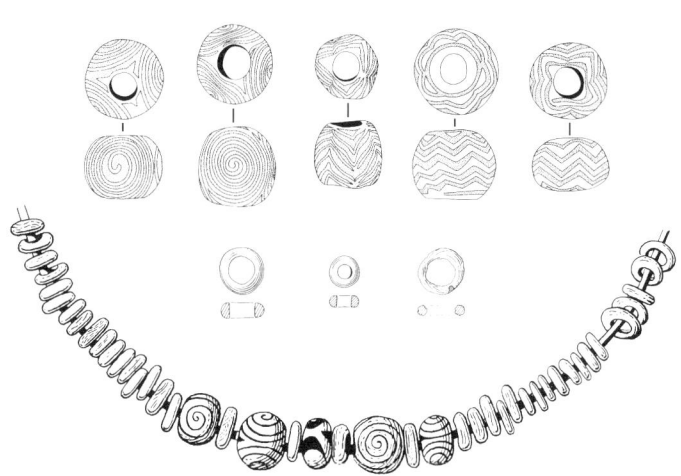

37. Glass beads made at Meare; the necklace (reconstructed) is from Meare Village East.

glass leaving only the inlay. The polished condition of some beads shows the use of the latter technique.

Widespread occurrence of Meare-produced beads within the site suggests that a part of the output was for home use. Amongst the finds were two necklaces, one of 45 beads (fig. 37), the other 17 beads. Although not common, Meare-made beads have been found elsewhere. Most have come from within a 100 kilometre radius of the source but Meare beads have been found as far afield as Cornwall and the Grampian area of Scotland. Doubtless it took some time for the beads to reach these destinations, involving a variety of exchange processes.

There was just a single Meare-made bead amongst the Glastonbury Lake Village glass. The duration of bead production at Meare is unknown but was possibly quite short-lived. The paucity of Meare beads at Glastonbury may be because the latter settlement did not come into existence until shortly after bead making at Meare had ceased.

Twenty-five glass beads were found at Glastonbury Lake Village, far more modest in number but more exotic than those from Meare. None was made in the settlement but at least 50% were continental imports - blue beads with white spiral decorated bosses, beads of brown and purple glass with whirl decoration, and plain ring beads. A few such beads were found at Meare which also yielded a fragment of glass armlet of a type rarely found in this country and again of continental origin. These imports were not the result of direct trade between the Lake Villages and the continental source, but would have arrived via a complex route. They may have entered Britain via Hengistbury Head, Dorset, a major port in the late Iron Age. Together, Glastonbury and Meare have produced one of the largest concentrations of imported glass beads in the country.

Shale and other stone

Shale objects were found in unusually large numbers, especially at Meare. Most of the shale was in the form of armlets but there were smaller numbers of rings, beads, vessel fragments and spindle whorls. Some armlets were very finely decorated including one with a series of oval-shaped pieces of sheet bronze rivetted to the outer face.

Shale is a soft, easily worked grey stone which was generally finished off by polishing to a shiny surface. The raw material was derived from the Kimmeridge area of Dorset. Finds from the source region show that the shale was exported as a raw material, as partially prepared rough-outs and as finished products (fig. 38). We cannot be certain whether the finished objects found at Meare and

38. Rough-outs and finished objects of shale from Meare Village West. Photograph by Lawrence Bostock.

Glastonbury were made on-site or were brought in. The unfinished knife or flint-cut rough-outs may have been worked from a block of shale on-site or they may have arrived in that condition to be finished off; either way they demonstrate shale working at both Meare and Glastonbury. Use of a lathe for shale working is evidenced by a single lathe core from Glastonbury. This is a flat disc with two holes on one side and was the means by which a piece of shale was attached to a lathe for turning. Lathe-turned shale objects found at the Lake Villages include the vessels and some of the armlets, though they were not necessarily all made there.

Most of the occupants' requirements for stone for other purposes - whetstones, querns, polishers, grinding stones and hammerstones - were met from within a radius of about 25 kilometres. Beach pebbles from the Severn shore were extensively used as whetstones and polishers and had the advantage that they required no modification to their shape before they were suitable for use. The nearby Burtle Beds were probably the source of slingstones which were found in the greatest numbers at Meare. The Mendip Hills were the primary source of stone for querns and hammerstones.

Clothing, ornamentation and games

With such a variety and wealth of products, it is tempting to see the people of Glastonbury and Meare as finely-clad and richly decorated on special occasions, and clothed more modestly for ordinary day-to-day activities (fig. 39). We do not have the evidence for these pictures, because the excavators did not find, or recognise, any textiles whatsoever; such fragile material, woollen fabrics possibly dyed

brown, reddish or yellow, may have survived as soft smears or pads of substances little different in colour or texture from the clays, peats, leaves or black earths of the sites. Clothing of leather, or of uncured animal skin, including furs, was also undoubtedly present on the sites but was not recognised; Bulleid in particular looked for the traces but nothing was recorded. The bones of fur-bearing animals such as beaver, otter, weasel and wildcat suggest that some people kept warm and were impressively-clad with fur coats, wraps, scarves or tassels. And it is probably not unreasonable to suggest that the colourful feathers of sea eagle, ducks and other birds sometimes adorned certain individuals.

Some of the bone and bronze needles found could well have been used in making clothing and in attaching the various fastenings and decorative features. Bronze brooches were used as fasteners for clothing as were bone and antler toggles (fig. 40). Blue, yellow, green, purple and brown glass beads were worn. A select few possessed amber beads whilst others wore perforated tusks of wild boar. Many people wore finger rings of bronze or iron usually in the form of a spiral. Some of these rings had a large diameter and may have been worn on toes. Bracelets of shale and bronze were worn; some of the former had been carefully repaired to extend their life. Other personal items included tweezers and, from Glastonbury, a bronze mirror.

39. Clothing from the Iron Age sites, a reconstruction mostly based on finds from Denmark, as no textiles were found at Glastonbury or Meare. Drawn by Jane Brayne.

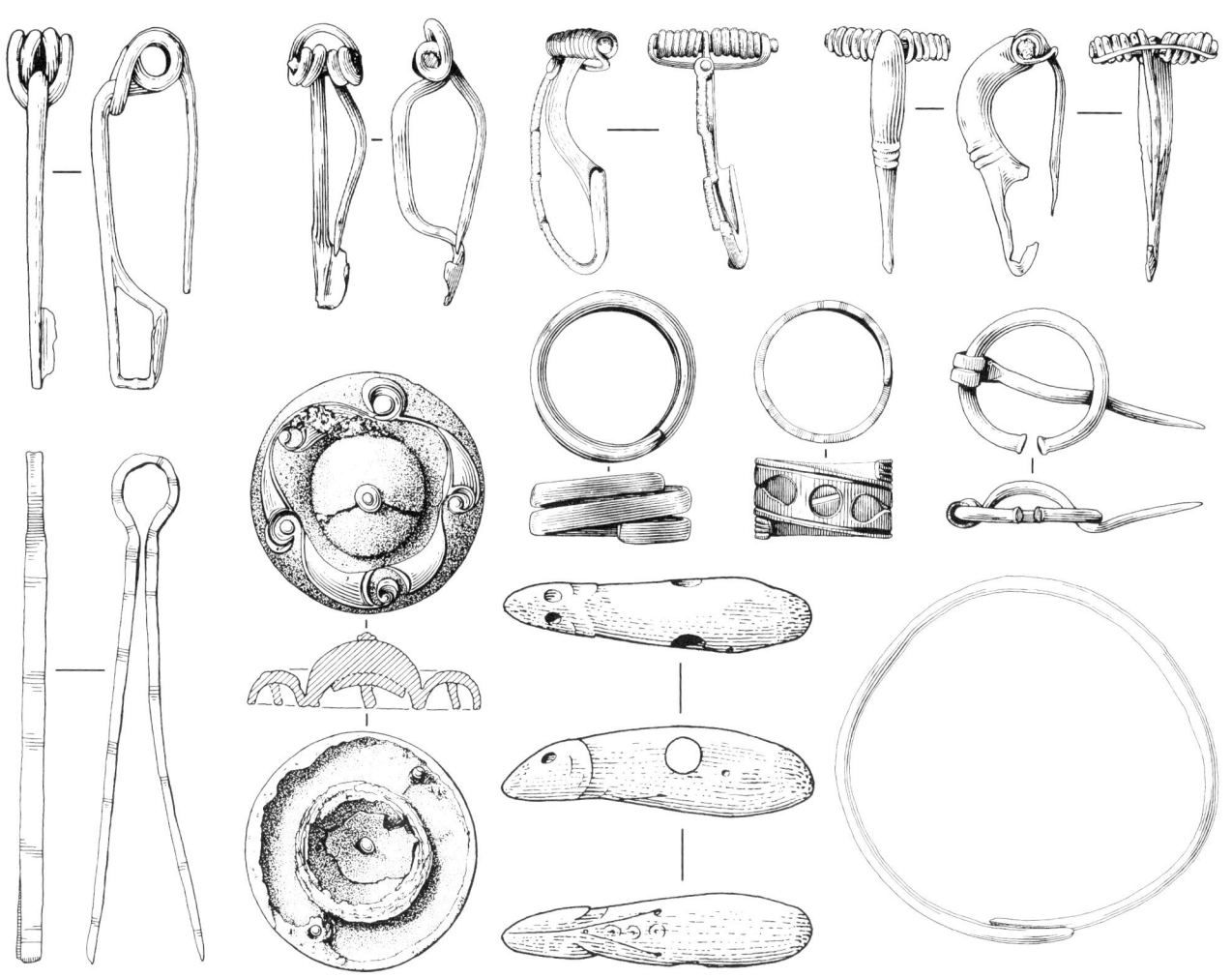

40. *Personal objects from Meare Village East; brooches, finger rings, tweezers, decorative mount, bracelet and a decorated antler toggle. Drawn by Mike Rouillard. Actual size.*

Although we know nothing about what form they took, the inhabitants doubtless enjoyed games of various kinds. The one clue that we have is a number of dice. All dice were of bar shape, made of antler and bone, and had only four sides on which dots could be incised. In all cases numbers one and two were omitted and the numbers ran from three to six (figs. 41 and 42). A series of square bone objects was found at Meare, possibly gaming pieces. Small

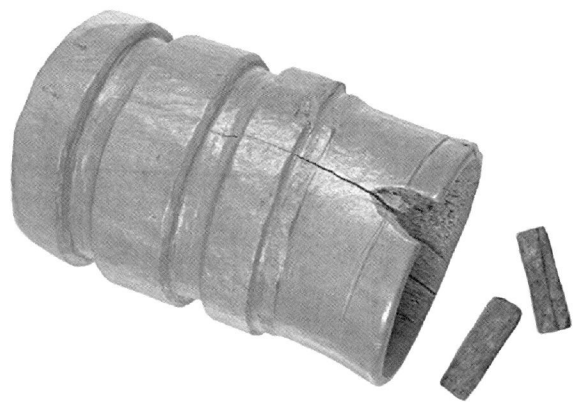

41. Dice and possible bone dice box from Glastonbury Lake Village. Photograph by Lawrence Bostock.

groups of smooth round pebbles may once have been counters. We do not know what form of game the dice were used for, whether it was serious gambling or for pure harmless pleasure. We may wish to imagine valuable ornaments, pieces of clothing, animals, weapons or tools being handed-over as a result of a bad throw of the dice, and some writers have included women as the prize, in fictitious accounts of a Celtic event. There is certainly no direct evidence to support such scenarios.

There must have been other games and amusements for both adults and children that have left no trace. It is unfortunate that nothing was seen or recorded at Glastonbury for children's toys or for music-making instruments; surely whistles, pipes and beaters or drums were present, but these might have been hard to identify. Even a length of reed or straw, cut carefully, can act as a pipe, and would be archaeologically invisible. The Lake Villages had provided good conditions for the preservation of materials and objects not normally, or ever, seen on other Iron Age sites, but there are still many aspects of ordinary life that are missing.

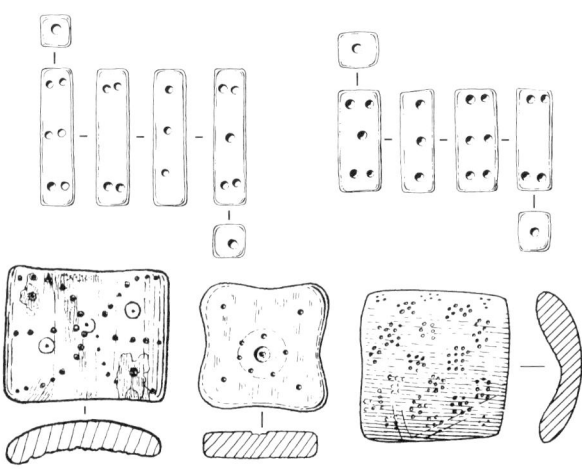

42. Drawings of dice showing the relationships of the numbers, and other gaming pieces. All are made from antler and come from Meare Village East. Dice drawn by Mike Rouillard.

DATES OF THE SITES

Dating of the occupations at Meare and Glastonbury is based on a combination of radiocarbon dating and the presence of distinctive types of artifact whose broad date range is known from studies elsewhere. The latter include brooches, coins, glass beads, imported pottery and to a lesser extent technological innovations such as the use of the lathe for wood and shale working. Together these provide a reasonably consistent guide to the dates of the sites. Meare began about 300 BC with activity focussed in the west. The eastern area came into use a few decades later. Glastonbury Lake Village was established slightly later around 250 BC. Thereafter the sites ran in tandem, all coming to an end around the middle of the first century BC. Hopefully the future may see the successful application of more precise dating methods to the sites such as dendrochronology (tree ring dating).

Both sites saw some very limited and enigmatic Roman activity. At Glastonbury, surviving traces amounted to just a few sherds of pottery. As well as a small quantity of pottery, Meare also produced five Roman brooches, a glass armlet fragment, a spoon and a number of coins. A concentration of 11 coins from one location probably represents the contents of a purse lost in the years AD 360 to 380. These finds certainly do not represent a continuation or revival of activity similar to that of the Iron Age. Instead they may be deposits relating to slight and sporadic use of the areas over the second to fourth centuries AD for purposes such as fishing, eeling, fowling or reed gathering.

THE INHABITANTS

We do not know where the inhabitants of Glastonbury and Meare came from nor very much about their physical condition. Cemeteries can often provide detailed information on the living - life expectancy, health, social status etc. No cemetery has been located for either Village. Home to many hundreds of people over time, a significant number must have died at Glastonbury and Meare. Either the cemeteries were sited on neighbouring dry land and have not as yet been traced or they practised methods of disposal of the dead which did not involve burial. Excarnation, exposure of the body to the elements for a period of time, is one possibility and has been proposed for other Iron Age communities where evidence for inhumation and cremation is absent. Such practice is not uncommon in modern non-industrial societies where a frequent custom is for part of the remains to be taken back to the settlement. Glastonbury and Meare, in common with other sites in southern Britain, produced a scatter of individual human bones and bone fragments - humerus, clavicle, tibia, tooth - which may have originated in this way.

A small number of burials was found within both settlements. Most of these were new-born infants, ten from Glastonbury and two from Meare. Some of these skeletons lay on or below clay floors. These infants provide the only identifiable evidence for the presence of children from both sites except for an object from Meare identified by Bulleid and Gray as a possible moss-lined wicker cradle. Reasonably complete remains of two adults were discovered at Glastonbury, one amongst foundation brushwood towards the southern end of the settlement and one from outside the palisade to the north west. No evidence for funerary ritual was recorded. In addition Glastonbury produced a single cremation which lay outside the palisade to the north east. Interestingly the burnt human bone was mixed with the charred remains of cow, pig, sheep or goat and probably frog. Animal offerings of this sort found in association with cremations are a well known feature of the European late Iron Age.

In common with the scatters of individual human bones from other sites of the period, the Meare and Glastonbury group includes a preponderance of skulls, whole and fragmentary. At Glastonbury most of these were found close to the palisade, both inside and outside the settlement. Four complete and particularly well-preserved adult skulls were discovered, at least one that of a woman. All bore between one and four cut marks, some very deep, inflicted with a sword (fig. 43). As none of these injuries shows signs of healing they clearly occurred around the time of death and may well have been the actual cause. The fact that these skulls were complete indicates that they received different treatment from the other skull fragments on-site. The shiny, polished look of the bone also singles out these four skulls as does the fact that they were the only human bones at Glastonbury or Meare

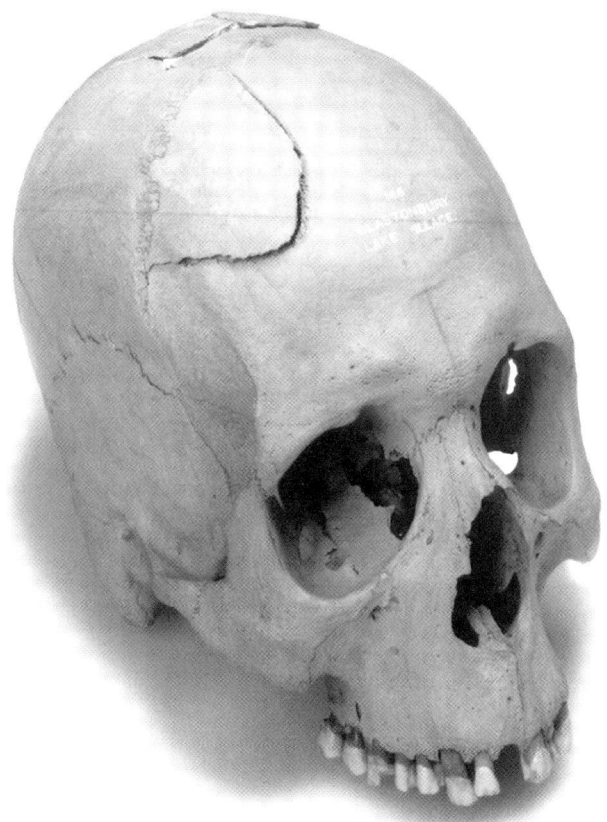

43. Human skull with sword cut from Glastonbury. Photograph by Lawrence Bostock.

48

44. Bronze sword scabbard found on Meare Heath in 1928. Photograph by Lawrence Bostock, drawing by Stuart Piggott.

with evidence for injury. The Celtic interest in the human head is well known and may be therein lies the explanation for these skulls. Glastonbury also produced a disc cut from a human skull which was given a central hole. This well-polished object was possibly worn as an amulet.

The presence of the sword-cut skulls shows aggression, something for which the Celts have a reputation. The original excavation report used the sword-cut skulls and scatter of bones to argue that Glastonbury Lake Village came to an end as the result of a massacre. Examination of the contexts from which the various bones came shows that their deposition spans the duration of the settlement and was certainly not the result of a single catastrophic event. Overall, the evidence from Glastonbury and Meare does not support the idea that warfare was of major concern to the inhabitants. The palisade at Glastonbury, whilst it could have served as a defensive structure, was there primarily to stabilise the

foundations. Meare had no such surrounding structure. A few items of weaponry were found at both sites - 13 iron spearheads, 5 daggers and a small quantity of shield edge binding. Sling shot, which occurred in quantity, could have been used for warfare or defence but could equally well have been used for hunting. We are left with little sense of threat or military tension. The most significant item of weaponry, a fine bronze sword scabbard, was found in 1928 on Meare Heath 2 kilometres directly south of the Meare Villages (fig. 44). Although not from the site itself it is certainly contemporary with its occupation.

Harness and bridle fittings found at Glastonbury and Meare, including bronze belt links and strap fasteners, show the use of horses. These animals were also represented amongst the bone assemblage but their role in the life of the settlement is not known. Certainly they would have found the conditions on-site uncomfortable. They were probably tethered here for short periods only, led through the shallow waters to the drier islands or uplands, and pastured on the grasslands. One of their tasks may have been to pull ploughs or carts, but it is likely that their place in society was also to be ridden out to the hunt, the exploration or the fight, and their presence at the settlements may have been for grooming and preparation prior to an expedition. Horses were a measure of wealth, and their ownership a signifier of status. The fine workmanship of the metal and bone harness-fittings and embellishments suggests pride in the appearance of the animal.

We are left, at the end of this description of the objects, industries and human remains, with a sense of both knowing these people and yet being almost completely ignorant about their lives. We can see the things they made, and what trinkets they wore, but we don't know any specific individuals, any faces, any special persons, a leader, or the relationships of husbands and wives, their children, or the organisation of family groups. The site of Glastonbury does have a good record now of the number of households at any one time, and indeed of particular places on-site where events involving more than one household may have taken place (see below). But we still lack those signs and signals of humanity, of human presence and human emotions, that would illuminate their lives for us. We do have, however, an important component in a detail that is lacking from any other contemporary site in Britain.

FOOD

One of the features of the excavations at the Glastonbury Lake Village and the Meare Villages was the good preservation of food remains (fig. 45). Because the sites had been wet or at least damp during their occupations, and because all were overwhelmed by floodwaters soon after abandonment, vast amounts of general debris, the rubbish of settlement, were sealed and kept wet over the centuries. When Bulleid found the sites, the drainage of the Brue valley was still underdeveloped, and he and Gray were in a position to recover all kinds of organic material. Some of their workmen were often skilled in recognition, able to see small wooden objects, slender fish and bird bones, and scatters of seeds as they spaded away through the mounds. At times we are sure that the workmen were less observant than they might have been, but at other times Bulleid could record a wide range of food remains that are not often found on Iron Age sites.

Both Bulleid and Gray were, or soon became, experienced in the identification of bones and plant remains, but they also relied upon a small army of specialists from the British Museum and other institutions for the more precise analysis of delicate food remains. Several of these experts tried to persuade the excavators to sample the wet peaty soils outside the settlements in the expectation of discovering major and deep middens, but this exploratory work could not be carried out in a systematic manner. Nonetheless, from all three sites there was recovered a quite remarkable array of foodstuffs. In several places, Bulleid's men came upon enough animal bone to fill several wheelbarrows, and berries or other seeds sufficient to fill a number of buckets. Here and there the men came upon small heaps of plant debris, or small piles of bones, each representing a deliberate act of dumping the residues of crop processing or animal butchery, or perhaps the remains of a feast. The bones in particular must have been well-sorted and dispersed by the settlement dogs here and there, but the general impression on all the three sites is that the people were seemingly

45. *Pottery from the Glastonbury Lake Village. The majority of vessels from Glastonbury and Meare were connected with the storage, preparation or serving of food. Drawn by Sue Rouillard.*

51

content to live and work among the rotting heaps of food debris. At Glastonbury, the various piles of rubbish were often dumped at the edges of the settlement, but at Meare the debris was probably more randomly scattered. This difference may well reflect the ways in which the sites were occupied as we will note below.

The bone and plant remains are most conveniently described here as food debris, but it will be clear that some bones and antler pieces were gathered together for working into tools, such as points, bobbins, hammers and so on. Plant remains probably include certain species used for textiles, rope, dyes and the like. However, the bulk of bone and plant remains were probably food residues, and

these can be separated into two groups - domesticated and wild. The inhabitants of the Glastonbury Lake Village were well-placed to obtain a wide variety of both, but the people of the Meare settlements may have had to go further afield to collect the full range.

The landscape of the Glastonbury Lake Village was a mixture of wetland and dryland, as the drawing shows (fig. 46). Arable fields for wheat, barley and oats were laid out on the dry slopes of the Glastonbury upland and the sand islands to the north. Some hoe plots for vegetables such as Celtic beans and peas were probably worked on the lower slopes. At the junction of the land and swamp, reed beds were harvested, and wildfowl captured here and on the more open waters. The raised bog

arable fields

hoe plots

reed beds

wildfowl

birds and berries on the raised bog

fish and eel

wild plants at the margin

unmanaged woodland

coppice woodland

pasture and water meadows

46. *The landscape and its economic potential around the Glastonbury Lake Village. Drawn by Sue Rouillard.*

to the west of the Lake Village attracted grouse and supported berries. The swamp and sluggish waters of the Brue yielded eel, fish and frogs; beaver and otter were also present in clearer parts of the water system. The shallow waters and damp ground at the edge of the swamp encouraged a variety of wild plants. Seasonal drying of low-lying meadowland and upslope pasture supported sheep and cattle. Upslope of this was woodland, coppiced in places. Above was the forest, used for supplies of timber and also for hunting of deer and forage for pigs.

From the Meare settlements there were fewer of these elements near at hand, but the dry rock island of Meare held woodland and arable fields, and the embryonic Meare Pool had eel, fish, wildfowl and many plants; pasture for sheep in particular may have been farther afield on the Polden slopes.

From these local areas, and from the upper reaches of the River Axe and out to the coastal zone of the Bristol Channel, the inhabitants of the Lake Villages obtained a very wide range of foodstuffs. Bulleid and Gray's books on the Glastonbury Lake Village (1911 and 1917), and on Meare Village West (1948, 1953 and 1966), and our report on Meare Village East (1987) provide lists of the species of wild and domesticated plants and animals. We have very little evidence of quantities, relative to one another, except for a few species.

Glastonbury Lake Village

Almost all the bones were of sheep, with some cattle, pig, horse and dog. The wild animals included otter and beaver, red and roe deer, wild boar, fox, wildcat, weasel, marten and polecat; some of these were not eaten, we suppose, but killed for skin and fur. The wetlands also yielded many birds to the hunters' arrows, slingstones and nets. The report speaks of a marsh and mere haunted by flocks of pelicans, cranes, swans and ducks; the long species list also includes cormorant, heron and bittern, and identifies goldeneye, teal, pintail, shoveller, widgeon, tufted duck, scaup, pochard and merganser. Puffin may have been a stray from the coast. Sea eagle, barn owl, kite and goshawk were probably killed for feathers not food. Coot, rail and grebe would have been gathered in by the children of the village, lying in wait amidst the fringing reeds of the swamp. The eggs of many birds were collected. The waters themselves provided good fishing, and perch, shad, roach and trout were certainly caught, probably along with other species whose bones did not survive to be identified on the site. Eel bones were not found, but these do not preserve well and most were probably chewed up by humans or dogs. Frog bones have recently been identified from the site. The fish bones show some variation in the waters of the Brue valley. Perch would prefer the clear moving water of a major stream, and trout also needed good

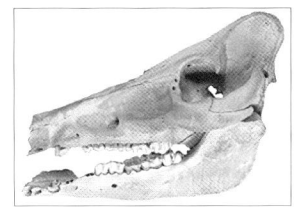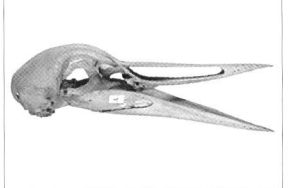

47. Evidence for diet: cow skull, pig skull, wheat, beans, crane skull, fish remains, sloe stones and hazelnut shells. Illustrations at varying scales. Photographs by Lawrence Bostock.

water; shad probably came from the estuary of the Axe or at least well north of the village. Roach was more local, in the muddy waters of the swamp (fig. 47).

But the food was not all meat or fish, and the plant remains are as remarkably varied as the animal. Wheat and barley were the most common cereals, and much was made in the excavation report of a lump of 'bread', consisting in fact of unbroken wheat grains mixed with some substance, perhaps honey, to make an unbaked cake 'kneaded on the palm of one hand with the fingers of the other, the hand being small and the fingers slender'; today we would not be quite so sure of the evidence. Along with the wheat and barley were Celtic beans and peas, and all were planted, tended and harvested on the dry islands and slopes to the north and south of the village. But the swamp and meadows also provided many wild plants, some gathered for food. About 40 plants were identified by Bulleid's specialists and the food plants include chickweed, parsnip, goosefoot, nettle, bulrush, bogbean, bur-reed, mustard, sloe, water lily and various berries and other fruits. Some of these were more edible than others, and their regular use as flavourings is not certain. There is no doubt, however, that the whole landscape was exploited in the search for and harvest of wild foodstuffs to accompany the domesticates (fig. 48).

The Meare Villages

Most of the bones identified from the two Meare villages were of sheep, with some cattle, pig, horse and dog. The species of wild mammals included red and roe deer, fox, otter

48. The interior of a round house at Glastonbury, with women at work and men arriving from the hunt. Drawn by A. Forestier, 1911.

and beaver, and wildcat. Bulleid and Gray did not record or collect animal bone as assiduously as they had at Glastonbury, but their specialist did identify over 30 species of birds, mostly marsh and diving birds and dabbling ducks. Among the birds are mallard, teal, widgeon, tufted duck, scaup, pochard, shoveller, sheldrake and goosander; cormorant, gull and gannet; red-throated diver; coot, rail and moorhen; crane and heron; partridge and grouse; falcon and kite. Some of these were probably killed as much for colourful feathers as for food and slender bones. The bones of salmon and roach, cod, perhaps bass, and eel were found in the Meare villages, some of them only recently identified from modern excavations and sieving of the deposits, or from re-examination of the Bulleid and Gray boxes of bone material. The eggs of snakes, and snail and limpet shells, were recovered in the early excavations. We might also mention that we found the bones of wood mouse, house mouse, water vole and field vole, none of them probably eaten by humans. And over 150 species of insects have recently been identified from Meare Village West, most of them beetles; perhaps some were considered edible, but more likely they were sheltering in the water vegetation around the site, or boring into wood, or living in the reed litter and other debris on and off the settlement.

Among the plant remains recovered in the early excavations, and supplemented by more recent work, are a wide variety of cereals. Emmer wheat, bread wheat and spelt, barley, rye and oats were brought to the site. Several buns of baked bread survive, burnt and discarded. The quantities of cereals were large; four wheelbarrows were filled with wheat by Bulleid's men from a place midway between the West and East villages. There were also quantities of beans and peas, and the bean weevil was at work on some of the food; its perforations and its actual remains have been found, one of the earliest records of the weevil in Britain. Wild plants were not seen or collected in the same abundance as at Glastonbury, but among them were various edible dryland plants such as fat hen and chess, and a number of mere or peat bog plants. Hazel nuts, sloe, elder and black berries formed part of the foodstuffs gathered on the sites. Taken as a group, the Meare Villages did not yield the wide varieties of wild plants and animals as did Glastonbury, but they had more types of cereals and the same preponderance of sheep bones.

The diet

With this great variety of plant and animal food potential at the Glastonbury and Meare villages, it is perhaps to be supposed that the inhabitants not only were well-fed on the usual Iron Age range of porridge and mutton, but were able to indulge in an extensive menu of different foods. We do not have any precise information about the recipes used in Iron Age kitchens, but it would be wrong to reject the possibilities of a very extensive menu offered to inhabitants and guests at the Glastonbury and Meare settlements. As we note below, visitors may well have been regular participants at activities on these sites, and what better welcome than to prepare and offer something a little out of the ordinary, something only available in such landscapes as the Glastonbury swamps and the Meare bog-side settlements. From experiences gained and experiments made in a number of wetland environments in Britain, France (especially) and elsewhere, we can speculate on what might have been possible for the Glastonbury cooks, in particular, to offer their fellows and guests. The menu is presented here as a guide to the potential, and all the ingredients were within the ambit of the Iron Age settlers, some acquired only by a journey to the coast, or the hills, but most readily to hand in the wetland and its margins (fig. 51).

49. Bronze figurine of a boar from Meare Village West. Boars' meat was doubtless enjoyed on occasion. Photograph by Lawrence Bostock.

50. The Glastonbury Lake Village seen from outside the palisade about 100 BC. Drawn by Jane Brayne.

57

MENU

Starters
Water cress soup made with duck stock, served with comfrey fritter
Sweet oar weed fried in nut oil and wild celery soup
Reed mace spikes and common mallow soup
Bean and duck egg salad with brooklime
Hazelnut cutlets with herb and kelp salad

Fish etc.
Tench cooked in crab apple juice with steamed laver
Smoked eel and wild celery
Pike steak and boiled marsh samphire
Terrine of eel and frogs' legs with nettle tips
Crayfish with herbs and waterlily tubers

Meat
Filet of heron and stewed nettle with brooklime salad
Wild boar cooked with bog myrtle berries and served with crab apple sauce and sea kale
Grouse or duck and cranberry bog sauce with sea beet and crab apple pickle
Beaver tail roast with hazelnuts, peas and comfrey sauce
Saltmarsh lamb and sea purslane with wild cabbage and meadowsweet
Roast swan with reed mace shoots and sea holly sweetmeats
Teal served with watercress and samphire

Sweet trolley
Goat cream cheese and honey
Reedmace pancakes with honey or apple jelly
Raspberries with cheeses
Bilberry crumble

Drinks
Beer: nettle, bog myrtle, sweet gale, crab apple cider
Wine: birch sap, oak leaf, elderflower, blackberry

Tea or coffee
Coffee: acorn, dandelion root, goosegrass
Tea: mint, limeflower, heather flower
(served with angelica crystallised fruits)

Afters
Fennel seed chews, willow bark aspirin, marshmallow chews

51. The Lake Village menu, using a wide variety of plants and animals from the environs of the Lake Village. Devised by John and Bryony Coles.

IRON AGE TERRITORIES

The Glastonbury Lake Village and the two Meare Villages were not the only Iron Age settlements in the region. The map shows the distribution of Iron Age sites that we know of today (fig. 52). The modest-sized hillforts of Dundon Hill (9 kilometres to the south), Maesbury (12 kilometres to the north east) and, further away, Westbury to the north and Brent Knoll in the west, ring the Levels. There is a scatter of settlements on the islands and hills, a cave site at Wookey Hole and a series of individual finds, mostly derived from the peat which in the closing centuries of the first millennium BC was a series of raised bogs. Our knowledge of the hillforts and settlements is limited, to the extent that we cannot be certain that all of these sites were contemporary with Meare and Glastonbury. Wookey Hole, 8 kilometres north east of Glastonbury Lake Village, is an exception. The presence of closely similar artifacts, including cordoned bowls imported from France, leaves no doubt that Wookey Hole was occupied at the same time as the Lake Villages; there may well have been direct contact between them. The ability to identify actual links between Meare and Glastonbury and other sites is limited at the present time though it is reasonable to assume that a network of links of various kinds existed.

Meare and Glastonbury were reliant upon the uplands and islands in their immediate locality for woodland, pasture, arable land, clay and stone. From slightly further away on the Mendip Hills came lead, decorated pottery and stone for querns. Stones for use as whetstones and polishers were carried from the Severn shore. From a greater distance came copper, tin, iron, shale and flint with some glass beads and pottery imported from the continent. Amber, originating from the Baltic and used for making beads, may also have been an import into Britain, or it may have come from amongst the small pieces occasionally washed up on the coasts of Scotland and eastern England. These exotic materials are most unlikely to have been direct imports to Glastonbury and Meare from long distance trade, rather they would have arrived via a succession of exchanges, some perhaps formal trading or bartering, others perhaps gift exchange or tribute. Contacts, direct and indirect, therefore ranged over great distances and contradict any assumption that might be made about people choosing to live in these apparently inhospitably wet conditions being isolated and marginal to the rest of society.

Much of the evidence found illustrates the essential self-sufficiency of the inhabitants: food production and preparation, metal working, cloth and clothing production, carpentry and bone and antler working. In return for raw materials not available locally

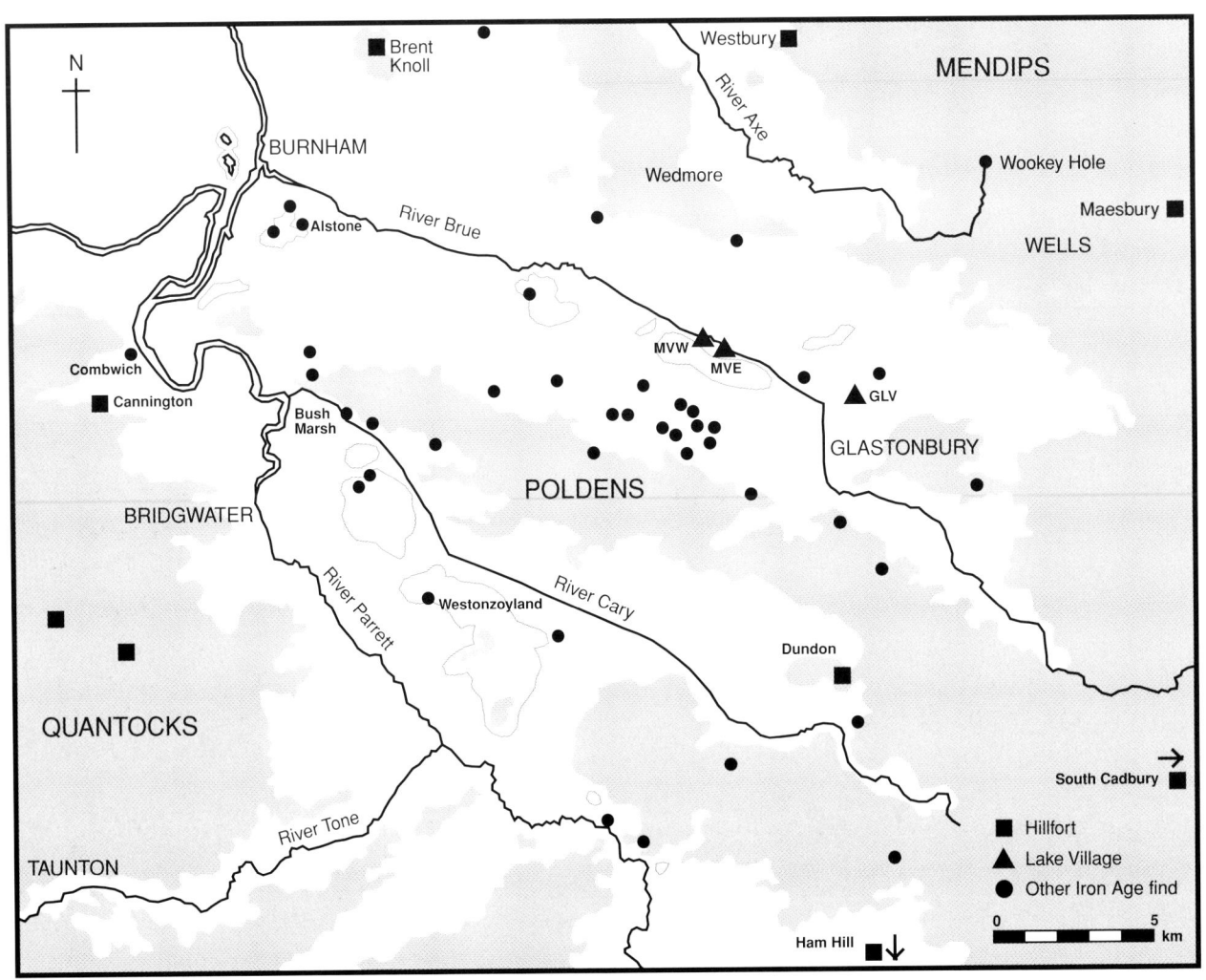

52. Map of the Somerset Levels with the Iron Age Lake Villages, hillforts and other finds shown. The shaded areas are over 15 metres above sea level. The dotted outlines are lower islands in the peat. The river courses shown are those of the present day. MVW= Meare Village West, MVE= Meare Village East, GLV = Glastonbury Lake Village.

and for objects of more distant origin the inhabitants must have generated surpluses or goods specifically for trade purposes. The two that can be identified from the archaeological record are glass beads from Meare and woollen cloth or even finished garments from both sites.

Does the exceptional quantity of finds from Meare and Glastonbury reflect their waterlogged condition and a correspondingly greater survival of artifactual evidence, or are they truly outstanding in this respect? There is no question that the presence of wood in such huge amounts, particularly at Glastonbury, is a direct result of the wet environment in which it had lain for over two thousand years. Other categories of find commonly occur on dry land sites; perhaps in the Somerset Levels they were more prone to loss in the damp conditions and therefore to survival. This may account for a proportion of the finds but presumably not those that lay on the many clay floors and work areas. The overwhelming impression is one of an abnormally large quantity and variety of finds from both Glastonbury and Meare. Certain objects such as the continental glass beads were doubtless prized and treasured possessions but overall the finds do not represent significant wealth; there are few outstanding pieces of metalwork, for example, nor does the distribution of finds identify the residence of anybody notably well off in terms of possessions. With few

exceptions the material is typical of finds from many dry land sites; it is the unusual concentration and range that is outstanding. This abundance of finds is emphasised when Meare and Glastonbury are compared with other late Iron Age sites in the area which have undergone some archaeological investigation, such as Westonzoyland, Alstone and Shapwick.

The Meare Market

What then was the nature or purpose of the sites? It has already been said that Meare, due to the strong likelihood of seasonal flooding, was probably only occupied for part of the year, at least so far as the majority of people were concerned. There may have been a few hardy souls who stayed throughout the year but most left for a drier location. This temporary form of occupation is reflected in the absence of substantial houses such as those found at Glastonbury.

Meare lay close to the boundary of the territories of two Iron Age tribes, the Durotriges of south east Somerset and Dorset and the Dobunni of north east Somerset and Gloucestershire. A third tribal area, that of the Dumnonii, lay a little to the west. The Brue valley was probably a convenient border zone, in the relative obscurity of a wetland. Here, land ownership may have been of less significance than on dry land where the demands and pressures were greater. Perhaps this area was politically neutral and therefore an ideal location for inter-tribal gatherings. It may well be that the occupation at Meare was seasonal not only for economic, environmental and seasonal reasons but also for social and political reasons. The wide variety and large quantity of artifacts may be evidence for annual or other regular gatherings of people from various places, providing them with an opportunity to meet, talk, settle disputes, barter and give and receive (fig. 53). The ample evidence for on-site production shows that these occasions were not simply for the bringing of goods for exchange but that craftspeople were very active also. These gatherings coincided not only with the time when the site was at its driest but also when the wild and farmed resources were at their peak. Food was abundantly available and we can very easily envisage feasting as part of these events. In circumstances such as these when people were only present for a relatively short period of time and in the warmest part of the year there would probably have been little need for permanent structures. All that was required to maintain the site in usable condition was the annual or periodic refurbishment of the clay platforms and hearths, with tents, shelters, windbreaks and enclosures being brought in or made on the spot as required. Gatherings such as these could have been very important in the establishment and maintenance of the economic, social and political relations of Iron Age communities in the region. In a complex rural economy as existed in this period, market centres were vital. Meare is one of very few sites in southern Britain which, it can be argued, existed primarily to fulfil such a function.

The Glastonbury Village

The wet but different environmental setting of Glastonbury and the fact that it was permanently occupied have been noted. However, the close proximity of it to Meare, the long overlap in their use and the similarity in the artifactual evidence argues for some kind of relationship between them. It may be that Glastonbury was an offshoot of Meare, a settlement established by a small group no longer happy with the seasonal arrangement at Meare and seeking somewhere more

53. One of only three Iron Age coins found at Meare and Glastonbury. This coin, 15mm in diameter, is from Meare Village East. Photograph by Lawrence Bostock.

permanent but still with the benefits of the wetland location. Perhaps the first settlers comprised a small group of minor specialists, their families and support groups. They may, for example, have felt that a more firmly-based industry was required to cater for sheep and its many products. Another difference between Meare and Glastonbury is that the evidence from the latter does not indicate any kind of temporary (seasonal) incoming of additional people, as would have been the case if it too was serving as a regional market or meeting place.

This then leaves us with further questions. Was Glastonbury a normal Iron Age site, permanently occupied, exploiting both wet and dry lands, but placed in a remote and inaccessible area for security as much as for resources? Was the village not normal at all but a specialised service settlement for industrial work by craftsmen and women who perhaps catered for the demands of other settlements in the region? Could the inhabitants have been the support or even the organisation behind the later gatherings at Meare? Abundant evidence for spinning and weaving suggests some expertise and skill but little from the site indicates full time or even necessarily part-time specialists; there was no glass making or working, limited iron forging and bronze working, some finishing of shale objects and of course carpentry. The impression is not one of a specialist workplace.

Was it a seat of local power situated in a low lying position surrounded by water rather than on a hill top protected by rampart and ditch, which was the norm for such a site in this period? Like the construction of massive hillfort defences, the artificial island at Glastonbury represents a large scale and protracted undertaking which probably involved at least a degree of social persuasion if not coercion. The abundance of artifacts may support this, the more exotic elements being perhaps from tribute or exchange. What, though, would the relationship have been with the nearby hillforts? On the other hand, maybe its low-lying position was meant to be unforbidding, even welcoming, easily accessible by water and politically neutral. These questions remain largely unanswered but at least illustrate some of the possible explanations for this remarkable site. Future work may provide some solutions. We do know that the settlement expanded over time from small beginnings and this would suggest that its role and significance in the wider world may have also changed.

One thing is clear. Some kind of authority lay behind the foundation and growth of the Glastonbury Lake Village. Decisions and control were involved in the original selection of a site, in the design and construction of the Village and its regular extensions, bearing in mind that all materials had to be transported in, in the siting and functions of the buildings and work areas, in the major reorganisations that took place. We do not know whether these decisions and organisational controls were exercised by an individual or by a group within the community. The distribution of finds suggests one or two locations where somebody of slightly greater wealth and therefore maybe authority lived. The most likely is an elongated building towards the southern end of the settlement, inside which the focal point was a clay table-like structure decorated by 67 incised circles, perhaps representing skulls or some other symbol of the group. Alternatively could this building have been some kind of a shrine? Besides the human skulls nothing of a ritual or religious nature has been identified. We are left with much evidence, many possibilities, and a number of puzzles.

The sites today

Some parts of the Glastonbury Lake Village remain unexcavated, including the lower levels of the elongated building and its decorated table, much of the Causeway or landing stage, some of the foundations, and various small parts of the site both inside and outside the palisade. Examination of some of these places, in the future, would allow the application of new techniques of recovery, analysis and dating, and might help us to interpret Bulleid and Gray's work more effectively. No other site in Britain matches the Lake Village, and its interpretation has to stand, or fall, on its own evidence. The same can be said of the Meare

occupations although here the concept of the seasonal market is better understood and the Meare sites may be considered unusual more by their setting than by their purpose. As a large amount of both Meare West and Meare East remains unexcavated, there are opportunities for future work to unravel some of the complex deposits on these sites, principally to understand better how the mounded areas developed, season by season.

The conditions of the three sites are now variable. The Glastonbury Lake Village (fig. 1) is essentially well-preserved, at least those parts left untouched by the activities of Bulleid and Gray; the surviving deposits are still wet, unploughed, intact. At Meare the conditions are not as good, because of drainage of the peat soils, machine levelling of part of the West site, and a more vigorous agricultural regime (fig. 54). All the signs at Meare suggest that the Iron Age deposits are degraded and will become less useful for the preservation of evidence as the years go by. Bulleid and Gray left many records of the Meare sites that remain unstudied, and we anticipate that modern analysis of these might allow new thoughts and opinions to be presented, along with new questions. The national importance of the three sites is indicated by their status as Scheduled Ancient Monuments.

When Bulleid was at work on his Glastonbury book, and digging at Meare, he often discussed

54. *The two Lake Villages at Meare (outlined in white). The modern course of the River Brue flows in from the east at middle right of the photograph and the modern village of Meare lies south of the two Lake Villages. Photograph courtesy of Somerset County Council Department for the Environment.*

the sites with his valued and elderly friend John Morland. They realised that there were many unanswered and unanswerable questions, and Morland commented once 'How one wishes they had been a lettered people'. But the people of the Lake Villages were not lettered, and we cannot hope to achieve the intimacy of detail and the names that a history might provide. Nonetheless we hope that what we have presented here will provide some answers, and offer some questions too, about the Lake Villages of Somerset.

55. A visitor to the Glastonbury Lake Village excavations in 1897.

References

The main published references to the Glastonbury and Meare Villages are:

Bulleid, A, 1926, *The Lake Villages of Somerset*.

Bulleid, A and Gray, H St George, 1911, *The Glastonbury Lake Village* Volume I.

Bulleid, A and Gray, H St George, 1917, *The Glastonbury Lake Village* Volume II.

Bulleid, A and Gray, H St George, 1948, *The Meare Lake Village* Volume I.

Coles, J M, 1987, *Meare Village East: The Excavations of A Bulleid and H St George Gray 1932 - 1956*.

Coles, J M, Goodall, A and Minnitt, S C, 1992, *Arthur Bulleid and the Glastonbury Lake Village 1892 - 1992*.

Coles, J M and Minnitt, S C, 1995, *'Industrious and Fairly Civilized'. The Glastonbury Lake Village*.

Gray, H St George and Bulleid, A, 1953, *The Meare Lake Village* Volume II.

Gray, H St George and Cotton, M A, 1966, *The Meare Lake Village* Volume III.

Collections

Collections and displays of material from Glastonbury and Meare:

The finds from Glastonbury Lake Village belong to the Glastonbury Antiquarian Society and those from the Meare Villages belong to the Somerset Archaeological and Natural History Society. The reserve collections from both sites are in the care of Somerset County Council Museums Service at Taunton and can be accessed by prior appointment. The excavation records and photographs for Glastonbury and Meare are held by the Somerset Record Office and the Somerset Archaeological and Natural History Society.

An exhibition of material from Glastonbury Lake Village can be seen at the Tribunal, Glastonbury, whilst a range of finds from Meare is on display at the Somerset County Museum, Taunton. The Peat Moors Visitor Centre, Westhay, features two replica Iron Age round houses based upon evidence from Glastonbury Lake Village.

Biographical details of the early excavators

Both Bulleid and Gray made enormous contributions to the archaeology of Somerset beyond their work at Glastonbury and Meare.

Arthur Bulleid (1862 - 1951)

Arthur Bulleid was born at Glastonbury. An interest in antiquarian matters had been instilled in him by his father but, unlike Gray, he received no formal training in archaeology. He learnt much from John Morland, also a Glastonbury man and one of the father figures of Somerset archaeology. Except for his early years at Glastonbury Lake Village, Bulleid's archaeological work was undertaken in his spare time; his professional career was as a general practitioner at Midsomer Norton. Work on Glastonbury and Meare occupied much of this 'spare time' but he also became involved in other fieldwork of his own as well as actively and financially supporting the work of others within the county. Bulleid's excavations and publications included the Roman villa discovered in Keynsham parish churchyard, an early Saxon cemetery at Camerton, a Bronze Age round barrow at Pool Farm, East Harptree, a Bronze Age timber trackway on Meare Heath as well as many other pieces of smaller-scale fieldwork. Bulleid was also heavily involved in the organisation and management of the Glastonbury Antiquarian Society and its Museum.

Harold St George Gray (1872 - 1963)

Harold St George Gray was born at Lichfield. His archaeological career began in 1888 when he was appointed as one of General Pitt-Rivers' assistants. He worked for Pitt-Rivers for some 10 years and in this capacity received some of the best archaeological training then available. In 1901, after a short period as Assistant Curator at the Pitt-Rivers Museum, Oxford, he became Secretary of the Somerset Archaeological and Natural History Society and Curator of the Somerset County Museum, owned and run by the Society. Until his retirement in 1949, Gray actively developed the museum and its collection. He also directed an extensive series of excavations on sites of many periods both within the county of Somerset and outside. Besides Glastonbury and Meare these sites included the Bronze Age Wick Barrow at Stogursey, the hillforts of Ham Hill, Cadbury Castle, Norton Camp and Kingsdown Camp, the medieval sites of Castle Neroche, Burrow Mump and Taunton Castle and the Neolithic henge monuments of Avebury (Wiltshire), Maumbury Rings (Dorset) and Arbor Low (Derbyshire).